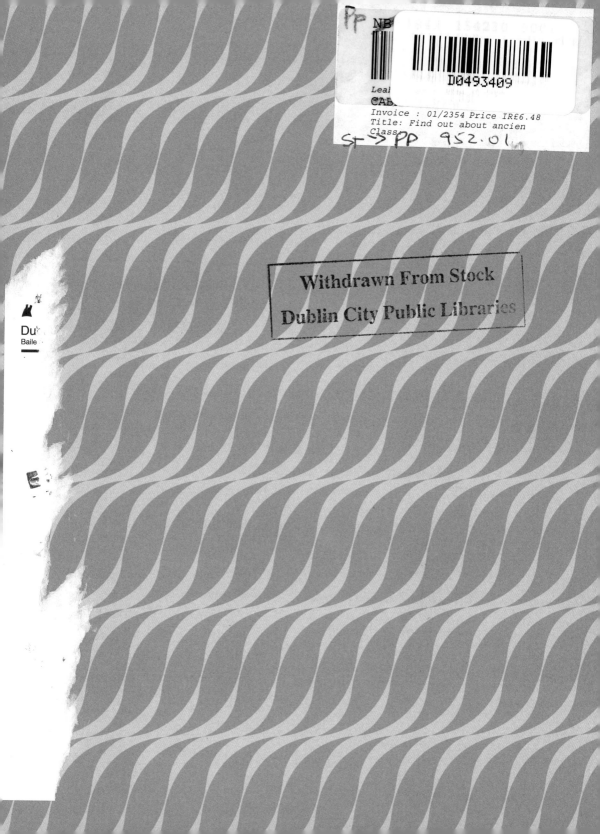

FIND OUT ABOUT

ANCIENT
JAPAN

Fiona Macdonald

CONSULTANT – Heidi Potter, Japanese Festival Society

southwater

This edition is published by Southwater

Southwater is an imprint of
Anness Publishing Limited
Hermes House
88–89 Blackfriars Road
London SE1 8HA
tel. 020 7401 2077
fax 020 7633 9499

Distributed in the USA by
Anness Publishing Inc.
27 West 20th Street
Suite 504
New York
NY 10011
fax 212 807 6813

Distributed in the UK by
The Manning Partnership
251–253 London Road East
Batheaston
Bath BA1 7RL
tel. 01225 852 727
fax 01225 852 852

Distributed in Australia by
Sandstone Publishing
Unit 1
360 Norton Street
Leichhardt
New South Wales 2040
tel. 02 9560 7888
fax 02 9560 7488

Publisher: Joanna Lorenz
Senior Editor: Nicole Pearson
Editor: Nicola Barber
Editorial reader: Richard McGinlay
Designer: Caroline Reeves
Illustration: Rob Ashby, Stuart Carter and Shane Marsh
Special Photography: John Freeman
Stylist: Thomasina Smith
Production Controller: Don Campaniello
Picture Researcher: Adrian Bentley

Anness Publishing would like to thank the following children for
modelling for this book: Sarah Bone, Otis Harrington, Rachel Herbert,
Joshua Parris-Eugene, Levinia de Silva,
Nicky Stafford, Kirsty Wells, Tyrene Williams.

PICTURE CREDITS

b=bottom, t=top, c=centre, l=left, r=right

Ancient Art and Architecture Collection: 17b, 19tl, 23br, 41tl, 42tl; E. Beintema/AAA
Collection: 22cl; Ronald Sheridan/ AAA Collection: 23bl, 35tl; AKG London: 1, 4br,
9br, 14tl, 35tl, 49tl, 50br; Heather Angel: 61br; BBC Hulton: 29c; Bridgeman Art
Library, London: The Life and Pastimes of the Japanese Court 13tl; Sumo Wrestler
Abumatsu Rokuunsuki by Kunisada 20tl, Fuji on a Fine Day by Kuniyoshi 23tl, Oxen of
the Kagaya Serving Tea by Harunobu 25bl, The Moon by Kunisada 28, Woman by
Kokumaru 35bl, Standing Courtesan by Kaigetsudo 36br, Collecting Insects by
Harunobu 37tl, Salt Maidens by Harunobu 38tl, Threading a Needle by Chinnen 39tr,
Tales of Bunsho by Tosa 45tl, Tale of Genji by Tokugawa II 46br, Courtesan with
Musical Instrument by Kuniyoshi 48tl; Urban Life 49tr, Ships Returning to Harbour by
Gakutei 51tr, The Stone Bridge by Hiroshige III 51bl, Retreat in the Mountains by
Toinioka 51bt, Woodblock by Yoshitaki 52br, Yokohama Seascape 53br, View of Dutch
Trading Post 53cl, Fuji in Fine Weather by Hokusai 55tl, Nichenen Calming the
Storm by Yoshimoro 56bl, Juraku Rakan 56tl, Cherry Blossoms at Asakura by Hiroshige
II 61tl; The following Bridgeman Art Library images are reproduced by kind permission
of the Fitzwilliam Museum, Cambridge: Mother Dressing Son by Harunobu 26tl,
Celebrated Beauties by Utamaro 36tl, Sudden Shower by Hiroshige 39br, Painting Party
by Kunisada 43cr, Fuji from Koshigaya 43cl, Mother and Baby Resting by Kunimaru
50tl; Christies Images: 3, 13bl, 16 bl & br, 17tl, 19bl, 23cl, 27br, 29bl, 35br, 37tr,
40br, 41tr, 44br, 53tr, 57c r & cl, 60tl, 60br: Bruce Coleman 55bl; Asian Art and
Architecture Inc: Corbis: 46tl, 47tl, Corbis-Bettman: 11cl, Carmen Redondo/ Corbis:
58br, Hulton-Deutsch/ Corbis: 21tr, Sakamoto Photo Research Laboratory/ Corbis: 28tl,
37bl, 47br, 57br, Seattle Art Museum/ Corbis: 21bl, Michael S Yamashita/ Corbis: 32bl;
CM Dixon: 10tl, 34tl, 45bl; Edimedia: 24bl, 26br, 38br; ET Archive: 4tl, 9tl, 11br,
12bl, 20br, 27tl, 42br, 51tr, 52tl; Mary Evans: 27bl, 34bl; Werner Forman: 10bl, 15cr,
15bl, 53cl, 59tl, 40tl, 49lc; Garden Picture Library: 57bl & bt; Michael Holford: 8br,
16tl, 18br, 22bl, 45br, 58tl; Hutchison/Jon Burbank: 43cl, 54tl, 57cl; Hutchison/
JG Fuller: 54bc; Hutchison/ Patricio Goycoolea: 39bl; Hutchison/ Chiran Kyushu: 29cr,
39bl, Hutchison/ Michael Macintyre: 12tl, 31bl, br; The Idemitsu Museum of Arts:
19cl, 37cl, 41cl; Images Colour Library: 33tr, 57bl; Japan Archive:
2, 5tl & bl, 8tl, 9tc, 11tr & cr, 13tr, 14br, 15tl & tr, 17tr, 18tl, 20bl, 30bl, 31tr, 32tl,
33tl, 33bl, 43tl, 48br, 53tr, 59tr; NHPA: 61c; Tony Stone: 58bl; Superstock: 58bl.

Previously published as Step Into Ancient Japan

CONTENTS

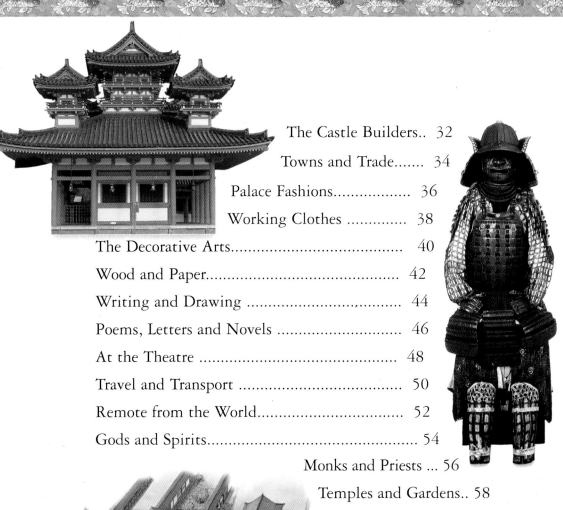

The Land of the Rising Sun

IMAGINE YOU COULD TRAVEL BACK in time 32,000 years. That was when the first settlers reached Japan – a chain of islands between the Asian mainland and the vast Pacific Ocean. On their arrival, the early settlers would have encountered a varied and extreme landscape of rugged cliffs and spectacular volcanoes. Over the centuries, a distinctive Japanese civilization grew up, shaped by this dramatic environment. The Japanese people became experts at surviving in a harsh land. Emperors and shoguns, feuding samurai and peasant workers all played their part in the history of these islands. Many castles, temples, inventions and works of art have survived from the past to tell us what Japanese life was like in ancient times.

ANCIENT POTTERY
This decorated clay pot was made by Jomon craftworkers around 3000BC. The Jomon people were some of the earliest inhabitants of Japan. Jomon craftworkers were probably the first in the world to discover how to bake clay in fires to produce tough, long-lasting pots.

EARLY SETTLERS
The Ainu people live at the northern tip of Japan. They look unlike most other people in Japan, and speak a different language. Historians believe that they are probably descended from early settlers from Siberia.

TIMELINE 30,000BC–AD550

From around 30,000BC onwards the Japanese islands have been inhabited. For long periods during its history, Japan was isolated from the outside world. In 1854 that isolation came to an end.

c.30,000BC The first inhabitants of Japan arrive, probably across a bridge of dry land, from the continent of Asia.

c.20,000BC Sea-levels rise and the Japanese islands are cut off from the rest of the world.

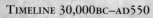
early pottery

c.10,000BC The JOMON PERIOD begins. The Jomon people are hunter-gatherers who live mainly on the coasts. The world's first pottery is invented in Japan.

c.3000–2000BC People from the Jomon culture move inland. They begin to grow food crops.

c.2000–300BC The Jomon people move back towards the coasts and develop new sea-fishing techniques.

rice fields

c.300BC The YAYOI PERIOD begins. Settlers from South-east Asia and Korea arrive in Japan, bringing knowledge of paddy-field rice cultivation, metalwork and cloth-making techniques. Japanese society is transformed from wandering groups of hunters and gatherers. Communities of farmers live together in settled villages.

Yayoi bell

30,000BC   10,000BC   500BC   AD300

DAIMYO AND SAMURAI

A samurai swordsman is shown locked in mortal combat in this woodblock print. Daimyo (noble warlords) and samurai (highly trained warriors) played an important part in the history of Japan. Daimyo controlled large areas of Japan (domains), and served as regional governors. Samurai helped them to keep control of their lands, and fight rival warlords.

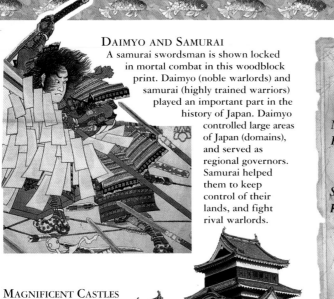

MAGNIFICENT CASTLES

During the 1500s and 1600s, Japanese craftworkers built many magnificent castles. This one at Matsumoto was completed in 1594–97. Originally, castles were built for defence, but later they became proud status symbols. They were signs of their owners' great power and wealth.

THE ISLANDS OF JAPAN

The four main islands of Japan stretch across several climate zones, from the cold north-east to the semi-tropical south-west. In the past, each island had its own character. For example, northerners were said to be tough and patient, people from the central region were believed to value glory and honour more than money, while men from the south were regarded as the best fighters.

---

*c.*AD300 KOFUN (Old Tomb) PERIOD begins. A new culture develops. New bronze- and iron-working techniques are invented. Several small kingdoms grow up in different regions of Japan. Rulers of these kingdoms build huge mound-shaped tombs. There are wars between the kingdoms.

花刺蟲飛

Chinese writing

*c.*AD400 The Chinese method of writing arrives in Japan. It is brought by Buddhist scholars and monks who come from China to work for the emperors of Japan.

*c.*AD500 The YAMATO PERIOD begins. Kings from the Yamato region become powerful. They gradually take control of large areas of Japan by making alliances with local chiefs. The Yamato rulers also claim spiritual power, by descent from the Sun goddess, Amaterasu. Calling themselves emperors, they set up a powerful imperial court, appoint officials and award noble titles.

Mount Fuji

royal tomb

AD400   AD500   AD550

Eastern Islands

JAPAN IS MADE UP of four main islands – Kyushu, Shikoku, Honshu and Hokkaido – plus almost 4,000 smaller islands around the coast. According to legend, these islands were formed when tears shed by a goddess dropped into the sea. The first settlers arrived on the Japanese islands about 30,000BC and by 10,000BC, a hunter-gatherer civilization, called Jomon, had developed there. At first, the Jomon people lived by the sea and survived by collecting shellfish and hunting animals. Later, they moved inland, where they cultivated garden plots. After 300BC, settlers arrived from Korea, introducing new skills such as rice-growing and iron-working. People began to live in rice-growing villages around AD300 and, in time, groups of these villages came to be controlled by local lords.

Around AD500, the rulers of Yamato in central Japan became stronger than the rulers of the other regions. They claimed the right to rule all of Japan, and to be honoured as emperors. These emperors built new cities, where they lived with their courtiers. However, by 1185 rule of the country had passed to the shogun (a military ruler). There were bitter civil wars when rival warlords fought to become shogun. In 1600, the wars ended when the mighty Tokugawa Ieyasu became shogun. For over 250 years the shogun came from the Tokugawa family. This family controlled Japan until 1868, when Emperor Meiji regained the emperor's ancient ruling power.

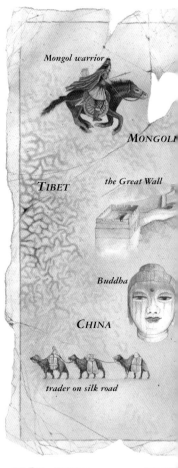

Mongol warrior

MONGOLIA

TIBET

the Great Wall

Buddha

CHINA

trader on silk road

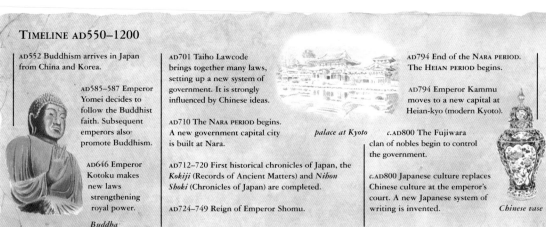

TIMELINE AD550–1200

AD552 Buddhism arrives in Japan from China and Korea.

AD585–587 Emperor Yomei decides to follow the Buddhist faith. Subsequent emperors also promote Buddhism.

AD646 Emperor Kotoku makes new laws strengthening royal power.

Buddha

AD701 Taiho Lawcode brings together many laws, setting up a new system of government. It is strongly influenced by Chinese ideas.

AD710 The NARA PERIOD begins. A new government capital city is built at Nara.

AD712–720 First historical chronicles of Japan, the *Kokiji* (Records of Ancient Matters) and *Nihon Shoki* (Chronicles of Japan) are completed.

AD724–749 Reign of Emperor Shomu.

palace at Kyoto

AD794 End of the NARA PERIOD. The HEIAN PERIOD begins.

AD794 Emperor Kammu moves to a new capital at Heian-kyo (modern Kyoto).

c.AD800 The Fujiwara clan of nobles begin to control the government.

c.AD800 Japanese culture replaces Chinese culture at the emperor's court. A new Japanese system of writing is invented.

Chinese vase

AD550   AD650   AD750   AD850

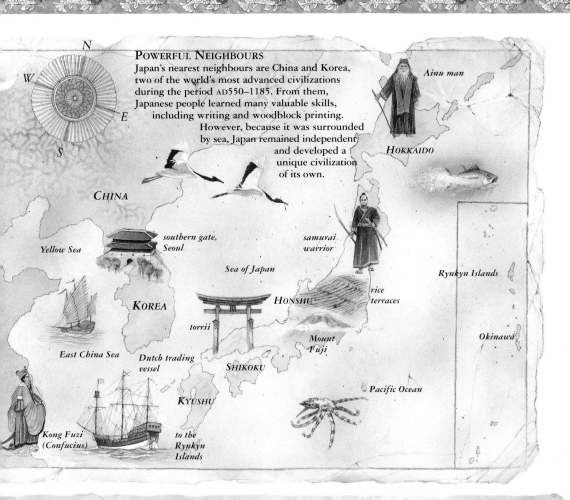

POWERFUL NEIGHBOURS

Japan's nearest neighbours are China and Korea, two of the world's most advanced civilizations during the period AD550–1185. From them, Japanese people learned many valuable skills, including writing and woodblock printing. However, because it was surrounded by sea, Japan remained independent and developed a unique civilization of its own.

Ainu man

N
W
E
S

HOKKAIDO

CHINA

southern gate, Seoul

samurai warrior

Yellow Sea

Sea of Japan

Rynkyn Islands

KOREA

HONSHU

rice terraces

torrii

Okinawa

East China Sea

Mount Fuji

Dutch trading vessel

SHIKOKU

Pacific Ocean

KYUSHU

Kong Fuzi (Confucius)

to the Rynkyn Islands

AD894 Links with China are broken.

*c.*AD900 The invention of new scripts for written Japanese leads to the growth of various kinds of literature. These works include collections of poetry, diaries, notebooks and novels. Many of the finest examples are written by rich, well-educated women at the emperor's court.

*c.*AD965 The birth of Sei Shonagon. Sei Shonagon is a courtier admired for her learning and for her witty and outspoken comments on people, places and events. She writes a famous pillow book (diary).

*c.*AD1000 *The Tale of Genji,* written by Lady Murasaki Shikibu, is completed. This was the story of love, politics and intrigue within the royal court. *The Tale of Genji* is one of the world's first novels. Lady Murasaki was the daughter of a powerful nobleman. She began to write after the death of her husband.

Lady Murasaki

AD1159 The Heiji civil war breaks out between two powerful clans, the Taira and the Minamoto. The Taira are victorious.

AD1185 Successive emperors lose control of the regions to warlike nobles. The HEIAN PERIOD ends. The Minamoto family, led by Minamoto Yoritomo, defeat the Taira. They gain control of most of Japan and set up a rival government at Kamakura, far from the imperial capital of Kyoto. Yoritomo takes the title of shogun.

Minamoto Yoritomo

AD1000   AD1100   AD1200

The Powerful and Famous

The History of Ancient Japan records the deeds of famous heroes, powerful emperors and bold warriors. Men and women who had won respect for their achievements in learning, religion and the arts were also held in high regard. In early Japanese society, royal traditions, honour, skill and bravery in battle were considered to be important, as was devotion to serious study. These principles mattered far more than the accumulation of wealth, or the invention of something new. Business people, no matter how successful, were in the lowest social class. However, during the Tokugawa period (1600–1868) many did gain financial power. Hard-working farmers, though in theory respected, led very difficult lives.

PRINCE YAMATO
Many stories were told about the daring adventures of this legendary hero. Prince Yamato probably never existed, but he is important because he symbolizes the power of Japan's first emperors. These emperors came from the Yamato region.

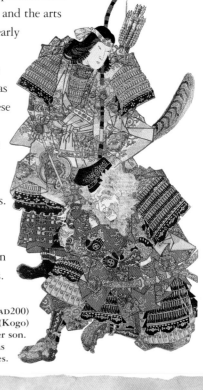

EMPRESS JINGU (ruled c.AD200)
According to Japanese legends, Empress (Kogo) Jingu ruled in about AD200, on behalf of her son. Many legends tell of her magic skills, such as her ability to control the waves and tides.

TIMELINE AD1200–1868

c.AD1200 Trade increases and a new coinage is developed. Zen Buddhism becomes popular during this period, especially with samurai warriors.

AD1274–1281 Mongols attempt to invade, but are driven back by storms.

samurai warrior

AD1331–1333 Emperor Godaigo tries to win back royal power. He fails, but his bid leads to a rebellion against the shogun.

AD1336 Ashikaga Takauji takes power and installs Emperor Komyo. He moves his court to Kyoto and encourages art and culture. Links with China are re-opened.

AD1338 Ashikaga Takauji takes the title shogun. The MUROMACHI PERIOD begins.

samurai swords

AD1467–1477 The Onin War – a civil war between rival nobles and provincial governors. The shogun's power collapses for a time. This is the first in a series of civil wars lasting until the 1590s. New daimyo (warlords) conquer vast territories in different regions.

AD1540 The first European traders and missionaries arrive in Japan. European traders hope to find spices and rich silks. European missionaries want to spread the Christian faith throughout Japan.

Portuguese sailor

AD1200   AD1300   AD1400   AD1500

TOYOTOMI HIDEYOSHI (1536–1598)
Hideyoshi was a famous war-leader. Along with two other great warlords, Oda Nobunaga and Tokugawa Ieyasu, he helped to unite Japan. The country was unified in 1590, after years of bloody civil war. As a peace measure, Hideyoshi banned everyone except samurai from carrying swords.

LADY MURASAKI SHIKIBU (*c.*AD978–1014)
The writer Lady Murasaki spent much of her life at the royal court as an attendant to Empress Akiko. Her book, *The Tale of Genji*, tells the story of the life and loves of Genji, a Japanese prince, in a sensitive and poetic style.

THE MEIJI EMPEROR (1852–1912)
The Meiji imperial family are shown in this painting. The emperor began his reign in 1867. The following year the shoguns' long period in office was ended when nobles (daimyo) engineered their downfall. The nobles then installed the emperor as a figurehead ruler.

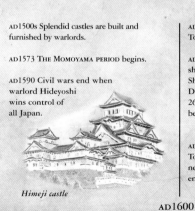

AD1500s Splendid castles are built and furnished by warlords.

AD1573 THE MOMOYAMA PERIOD begins.

AD1590 Civil wars end when warlord Hideyoshi wins control of all Japan.

Himeji castle

AD1600 MOMOYAMA PERIOD ends and the TOKUGAWA PERIOD begins.

AD1603 Tokugawa Ieyasu becomes shogun and rules all Japan. Shoguns from the TOKUGAWA DYNASTY rule Japan for the next 267 years. Edo (modern Tokyo) becomes the new capital.

Kabuki actor

AD1603 A long period of peace begins. Towns and trade expand and new popular forms of art and entertainment develop.

AD1853 and 1854 USA sends Black Ships to demand the right to trade with Japan.

AD1868 End of the TOKUGAWA PERIOD. Tokugawa shoguns lose power. Emperor Meiji is made head of state and begins a programme of modernization.

Commander Perry's Black Ships

AD1600

AD1800

God-like Emperors

THE JAPANESE PEOPLE began to live in villages in about 300BC. Over the next 600 years, the richest and most powerful of these villages became the centres of small kingdoms, controlling the surrounding lands. By about AD300, a kingdom based on the Yamato Plain in south-central Japan became bigger and stronger than the rest. It was ruled by chiefs of an *uji* (clan) who claimed to be descended from the Sun goddess. The chiefs of this Sun-clan were not only army commanders – they were priests, governors, law-makers and controllers of their people's treasure and food supply. Over the years, their powers increased. By around AD500, Sun-clan chiefs from Yamato ruled over most of Japan. They claimed power as emperors, and organized lesser chiefs to work for them, giving them noble titles as a reward. Each emperor chose his own successor from within the Sun-clan, and handed over to him the sacred symbols of imperial power – a jewel, a mirror and a sword. Sometimes, if a male successor to the throne was not old enough to rule, an empress would rule as regent in his place.

Descendants of these early emperors still rule Japan today. However, at times they had very little power. Some emperors played an active part in politics, but others spent their time shut away from the outside world. Today, the emperor has only a ceremonial role in the government of Japan.

HANIWA FIGURE
From around AD300 to AD550, hollow clay figures were placed around the edges of tombs. These figures, shaped like humans or animals, are known as Haniwa.

NARA
This shrine is in the ancient city of Nara. Originally called Heijokyo, Nara was founded by Empress Gemmei (ruled AD707–715) as a new capital for her court. The city was planned and built in Chinese style, with streets arranged in a grid pattern. The Imperial Palace was situated at the northern edge.

FANTASTIC STORIES

Prince Shotoku (AD574–622) was descended from the imperial family and from another powerful clan, the Soga. He never became emperor, but ruled as regent for 30 years on behalf of Empress Suiko. Many fantastic stories were told about him – for example, that he was able to speak as soon as he was born. It was also said that he could see into the future. More accurate reports of his achievements list his introduction of a new calendar, and his reform of government, based on Chinese ideas. He was also a supporter of the new Buddhist faith, introduced from China.

LARGEST WOODEN STRUCTURE

The Hall of the Great Buddha at Nara was founded on the orders of Emperor Shomu in AD745. The whole temple complex is said to be the largest wooden structure in the world. It houses a bronze statue of the Buddha, 16m tall and weighing 500 tonnes, and was also designed to display the emperor's wealth and power. There is a treasury close to the Hall of the Great Buddha, built in AD756. This housed the belongings of Emperor Shomu and his wife, Empress Komyo. The treasury still contains many rare and valuable items.

BURIAL MOUNDS

The Yamato emperors were buried in huge, mound-shaped tombs surrounded by lakes. The largest, built for Emperor Nintoku, is 480m long. From above, the tombs have a keyhole-shaped layout. Inside, they contain many buried treasures.

THE SUN GODDESS

The Sun goddess Amaterasu Omikami is shown emerging from the earth in this print. She was both honoured and feared by Japanese farmers. One of the emperor's tasks was to act as a link between the goddess and his people, asking for her help on their behalf. The goddess's main shrine was at Ise, in central Japan. Some of its buildings were designed to look like grain stores – a reminder of the Sun's power to cause a good or a bad harvest.

Nobles and Courtiers

I**N EARLY JAPAN**, everyone from the proudest chief to the poorest peasant owed loyalty to the emperor. However, many nobles ignored the emperor's orders – especially when they were safely out of reach of his court. There were plots and secret schemes as rival nobles struggled to influence the emperor and to seize power for themselves.

Successive emperors passed laws to try to keep their nobles and courtiers under control. The most important new laws were introduced by Prince Shotoku (AD574–622) and Prince Naka no Oe (AD626–671). Prince Naka considered his laws to be so important that he gave them the name Taika (Great Change). The Taika laws created a strong central government, run by a Grand Council of State, and a well-organized network of officials to oversee the 67 provinces.

BUGAKU
A Bugaku performer makes a slow, stately movement. Bugaku is an ancient form of dance that was popular at the emperor's court over 1,000 years ago. It is still performed there today.

POLITE BEHAVIOUR
A group of ladies watches an archery contest from behind a screen at the edge of a firing range. The behaviour of courtiers was governed by rigid etiquette. Noble ladies had to follow especially strict rules. It was bad-mannered for them to show their faces in public. Whenever men were present, the ladies crouched behind a low curtain or a screen, or hid their faces behind their wide sleeves or their fans. To protect their faces when travelling, they concealed themselves behind curtains or sliding panels fitted to their ox-carts. They also often left one sleeve dangling outside.

THE SHELL GAME
You will need: fresh clams, water bowl, paintbrush, gold paint, white paint, black paint, red paint, green paint, water pot.

1 Ask an adult to boil the clams. Allow them to cool and then remove the insides. Wash the shells and leave them to dry. When dry, paint the shells gold.

2 Carefully pull each pair of shells apart. Now paint an identical design on to each of a pair of clam shells. Start by painting a white, round face.

3 Add features to the face. In the past, popular pictures, such as scenes from the *Tale of Genji*, were painted on to the shell pairs.

NOBLES AT COURT

Two nobles are shown here riding a splendid horse. Noblemen at the imperial court spent much of their time on government business. They also practised their riding and fighting skills, took part in court ceremonies, and read and wrote poetry.

THE IMPERIAL COURT

Life at court was both elegant and refined. The buildings were exquisite and set in beautiful gardens. Paintings based on the writings of courtiers show some of the famous places they enjoyed visiting.

THE FUJIWARA CLAN

Fujiwara Teika (1162–1241) was a poet and a member of the Fujiwara clan. This influential family gained power at court by arranging the marriages of their daughters to young princes and emperors. Between AD724 and 1900, 54 of the 76 emperors of Japan had mothers who were related to the Fujiwara clan.

A LOOK INSIDE

This scroll-painting shows rooms inside the emperor's palace and groups of courtiers strolling in the gardens outside. Indoors, the rooms are divided up by silken blinds and the courtiers sit on mats and cushions.

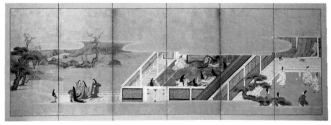

4 Paint several pairs of clam shells with various designs. Make sure that each pair of shells has an identical picture. Leave the painted shells to dry.

5 Turn all your shells face down and mix them up well. Turn over one shell then challenge your opponent to pick the matching shell to yours.

6 If the two shells do not match, turn them over and try again. If they do match, your opponent takes the shells. Take it in turns to challenge each other.

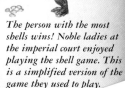

The person with the most shells wins! Noble ladies at the imperial court enjoyed playing the shell game. This is a simplified version of the game they used to play.

Shoguns and Civil Wars

IN 1159, a bloody civil war, known as the Heiji War, broke out in Japan between two powerful clans, the Taira and the Minamoto. The Taira were victorious in the Heiji War, and they controlled the government of the country for 26 years. However, the Minamoto rose again and regrouped to defeat the Taira in 1185.

Yoritomo, leader of the Minamoto clan, became the most powerful man in Japan and set up a new headquarters in the city of Kamakura. The emperor continued to act as head of the government in Kyoto, but he was effectively powerless. For almost the next 700 years, until 1868, military commanders such as Yoritomo were the real rulers of Japan. They were known by the title *sei i tai shogun*, an army term meaning Great General Subduing the Barbarians.

SHOGUN FOR LIFE
Minamoto Yoritomo was the first person to take the title shogun and to hand the title on to his sons. In fact, the title did not stay in the Minamoto family for long because the family line died out in 1219. But new shogun families soon took its place.

FIRE! FIRE!
This scroll-painting illustrates the end of a siege during the Heiji War. The war was fought between two powerful clans, the Taira and the Minamoto. The rival armies set fire to buildings by shooting burning arrows and so drove the inhabitants out into the open where they could be killed.

MAKE A KITE

You will need: A1 card, ruler, pencil, dowelling sticks tapered at each end (5 x 50cm, 2 x 70cm), masking tape, scissors, glue, brush, thread, paintbrush, paints, water pot, paper (52cm x 52cm), string, bamboo stick.

1 Draw a square 50cm x 50cm on card with a line down the centre. Lay the dowelling sticks on the square. Glue the sticks to each other and then tape.

2 When the glue has dried, remove the masking tape. Take the frame off the card. Bind the corners of the frame with the strong thread.

3 Now position your two longer dowelling sticks so that they cross in the middle of the square. Glue and then bind the corners with the strong thread.

DYNASTY FOUNDER

Tokugawa Ieyasu (1542-1616) was a noble from eastern Japan. He was one of three powerful warlords who brought long years of civil war to an end and unified Japan. In 1603 he won the battle of Sekigahara and became shogun. His family, the Tokugawa, ruled Japan for the next 267 years.

RESTING PLACE

This mausoleum (burial chamber) was built at Nikko in north-central Japan. It was created to house the body of the mighty shogun Tokugawa Ieyasu. Three times a year, Ieyasu's descendants travelled to Nikko to pay homage to their great ancestor.

UNDER ATTACK

Life in Nijo Castle, Kyoto, is shown in great detail on this painted screen. The castle belonged to the Tokugawa family of shoguns. Like emperors, great shoguns built themselves fine castles, which they used as centres of government or as fortresses in times of war. Nijo Castle was one of the finest buildings in Japan. It had 'nightingale' floors that creaked loudly when an intruder stepped on them, raising the alarm. The noise was made to sound like a bird call.

Kites were sometimes used for signalling during times of war. The Japanese have also enjoyed playing with kites for over 1,000 years.

4 Paint a colourful kite pattern on to the paper. It is a good idea to tape the edges of the paper down so it does not move around or curl up.

5 Draw light pencil marks 1cm in from the corners of the paper on all four sides. Carefully cut out the corners of the paper, as shown.

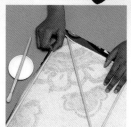

6 Glue the paper on to the kite frame. You will need to glue along the wooden frame and fold the paper over the edge of the frame. Leave to dry.

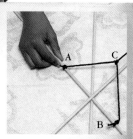

7 Tie a short length of string across the centre of the kite frame (A to B). Knot a long kite string on to it as shown (C). Wind the string on the bamboo.

Samurai

BETWEEN 1185 AND 1600 there were a great many wars as rival nobles (known as 'daimyo') fought to become shogun. Some emperors also tried, unsuccessfully, to restore imperial rule. During this troubled time in Japanese history, emperors, shoguns and daimyo all relied on armies of well-trained samurai (warriors) to fight their battles. The samurai were men from noble families, and they were skilled at fighting battles. Members of each samurai army were bound together by a solemn oath, sworn to their lord. They stayed loyal from a sense of honour – and because their lord gave them rich rewards. The civil wars ended around 1600, when the Tokugawa dynasty of shoguns came to power. From this time onwards, samurai spent less time fighting. Instead, they served their lords as officials and business managers.

RIDING OFF TO WAR
Painted in 1772, this samurai general is in full armour. A samurai's horse had to be fast, agile and strong enough to carry the full weight of the samurai, his armour and his weapons.

TACHI
Swords were a favourite weapon of the samurai. This long sword is called a *tachi*. It was made in the 1500s for ceremonial use by a samurai.

METAL HELMET
Samurai helmets like this were made from curved metal panels, carefully fitted together, and decorated with elaborate patterns. The jutting peak protected the wearer's face and the nape-guard covered the back of the neck. This helmet dates from around 1380.

SAMURAI HELMET

You will need: *thick card, pin, string, felt-tip pen, ruler, scissors, tape measure, newspaper, bowl, water, PVA glue, balloon, petroleum jelly, pencil, modelling clay, bradawl, paper, gold card, paints, brush, water pot, glue brush, masking tape, paper fasteners, 2 x 20cm lengths of cord.*

1 Draw a circle 18cm in diameter on card using the pin, string and felt-tip pen. Using the same method, draw two larger circles 20cm and 50cm.

2 Draw a line across the centre of the three circles using the ruler and felt-tip pen. Draw tabs in the middle semi-circle. Add two flaps as shown.

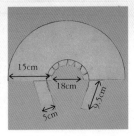

15cm
18cm
5cm
2.5cm

3 Now cut out the neck protector piece completely, as shown above. Make sure that you cut around the tabs and flaps exactly.

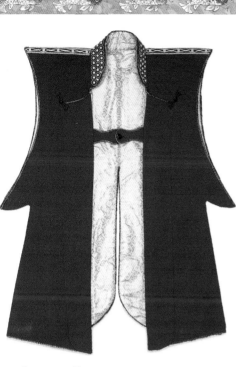

PROTECTIVE CLOTHING

This fine suit of samurai armour dates from the Tokugawa period (1600–1868). Armour gave the samurai life-saving protection in battle. High-ranking warriors wore suits of plate armour, made of iron panels, laced or riveted together and combined with panels of chain mail or rawhide. Lower-ranking soldiers, called *ashigaru*, wore thinner, lightweight armour, made of small metal plates. A full suit of samurai armour could weigh anything up to 18kg.

SURCOAT FINERY

For festivals, ceremonies and parades samurai wore surcoats (long, loose tunics) over their armour. Surcoats were made from fine, glossy silks, dyed in rich colours. This example was made during the Tokugawa period (1600–1868). Surcoats were often decorated with family crests. These were originally used to identify soldiers in battle, but later became badges of high rank.

MAKING BOWS

Japanese craftworkers are busy at work making bows, around 1600. The bow was the Japanese warrior's most ancient weapon. Bows were made of wood and bamboo and fired many different kinds of arrow.

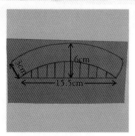

4 Draw the peak template piece on another piece of card. Follow the measurements shown in the picture. Cut out the peak template.

5 To make papier-mâché, tear the newspaper into small strips. Fill the bowl with 1 part PVA glue to 3 parts water. Add the newspaper strips.

6 Blow up the balloon to the size of your head. Cover with petroleum jelly. Build up three papier-mâché layers on the top and sides. Leave to dry between layers.

7 When dry, pop the balloon and trim. Ask a friend to make a mark on either side of your head.

Instructions for the helmet continue on the next page...

The Way of the Warrior

SAMURAI were highly-trained warriors who dedicated their lives to fighting for their lords. However, being a samurai involved more than just fighting. The ideal samurai was supposed to follow a strict code of behaviour, governing all aspects of his life. This code was called *bushido* – the way of the warrior. *Bushido* called for skill, self-discipline, bravery, loyalty, honour, honesty, obedience and, at times, self-sacrifice. It taught that it was nobler to die fighting than to run away and survive.

Many samurai warriors followed the religious teachings of Zen, a branch of the Buddhist faith. Zen was introduced into Japan by two monks, Eisai and Dogen, who went to China to study in the 1100s and 1200s and brought Zen practices back with them. Teachers of Zen encouraged their followers to meditate (to free the mind of all thoughts) in order to achieve enlightenment.

THE TAKEDA FAMILY
The famous daimyo (warlord) Takeda Shingen (1521–1573), fires an arrow using his powerful bow. The influential Takeda family owned estates in Kai province near the city of Edo and kept a large private army of samurai warriors. Takeda Shingen fought a series of wars with his near neighbour, Uesugi Kenshin. However, in 1581, the Takeda were defeated by the army of General Nobunaga.

SWORDSMEN
It took young samurai many years to master the skill of swordsmanship. They were trained by master swordsmen. The best swords, made of strong, springy steel, were even given their own names.

8 Place clay under the pencil marks. Make two holes – one above and one below each pencil mark – with a bradawl. Repeat on the other side.

9 Fold a piece of A4 paper and draw a horn shape on to it following the design shown above. Cut out this shape so that you have an identical pair of horns.

10 Take a piece of A4 size gold card. Place your paper horns on to the gold card and draw around them. Carefully cut the horns out of the card.

11 Paint the papier-mâché helmet brown. Paint a weave design on the neck protector and a cream block on each flap. Leave to dry.

OFF TO WAR

A samurai warrior (on horseback) and foot-soldiers set off for war. Samurai had to command and inspire confidence in others, so it was especially important for them to behave in a brave and honourable way.

MARTIAL ARTS

Several sports that people enjoy playing today have developed from samurai fighting skills. In aikido, players try to throw their opponent off-balance and topple them to the ground. In kendo, players fight one another with long swords made of split bamboo. They score points by managing to touch their opponent's body, not by cutting or stabbing them!

kendo   *aikido*

SURVIVAL SKILLS

Samurai had to know how to survive in wild countryside. Each man carried emergency rations of dried rice. He also used his fighting skills to hunt wild animals for food.

ZEN

The Buddhist monk Rinzai is shown in this Japanese brush and ink scroll-painting. Rinzai was a famous teacher of Zen ideas. Many pupils, including samurai, travelled to his remote monastery in the mountains to study with him.

Samurai helmets were often decorated with crests made of lacquered wood or metal. These were mounted on the top of the helmet.

12 Bend back the tabs on the peak piece. Position it at the front of the helmet. Stick the tabs to the inside with glue. Hold in place with tape.

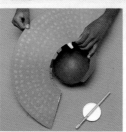

13 Now take the neck protector. Bend back the front flaps and the tabs. Glue the tabs to the helmet, as shown. Leave the helmet to dry.

14 Stick the horns to the front of the helmet. Use paper fasteners to secure, as shown. Decorate the ear flaps with paper fasteners.

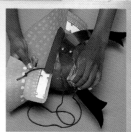

15 Thread cord through one of the holes made in step 8. Tie a knot in the end. Thread the other end of the cord through the second hole. Repeat on the other side.

Peasant Farmers

U NTIL THE 1900S, most Japanese people lived in the countryside and made a living either by fishing or by farming small plots of land. Japanese farmers grew crops for three different reasons. They grew rice to sell to the samurai or to pay taxes. Barley, millet, wheat and vegetables were used for their own food.

Traditionally, Japanese society was divided into four main classes – samurai, peasant farmers, craftworkers and merchants. Samurai were the most highly respected. Farmers and craftworkers came next because they produced useful goods. Merchants were the lowest rank because they produced nothing themselves.

During the Tokugawa period (1600–1868), society began to change. Towns and cities grew bigger, small industries developed and trade increased. Farmers began to sell their crops to people who had no land of their own. For the first time, some farmers had money to spend on better clothes, houses, and more food.

WRESTLERS
Sumo wrestling has long been a favourite sport in Japan. It developed from religious rituals and from games held at farmers' festivals in the countryside. Sumo wrestlers are usually very fat. They use their massive weight to overbalance their opponents.

RICE FARMING
Planting out tiny rice seedlings in shallow, muddy water was tiring, back-breaking work. Rice farming was introduced to Japan soon after 300BC. Most varieties of rice need to grow in flooded fields, called *tanbo* (paddy-fields). To provide extra food, farmers also reared fish in the *tanbo*.

TERRACING
It was difficult to find enough flat land for growing crops in Japan, so terraces were cut, like steps, into the steep hillsides. Farmland could be shaken by earthquakes or ruined by floods. In years when the harvests failed, there was often famine.

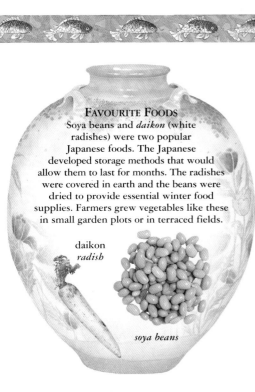

FAVOURITE FOODS

Soya beans and *daikon* (white radishes) were two popular Japanese foods. The Japanese developed storage methods that would allow them to last for months. The radishes were covered in earth and the beans were dried to provide essential winter food supplies. Farmers grew vegetables like these in small garden plots or in terraced fields.

daikon
radish

soya beans

A HARD LIFE

A woman farm-worker carries heavy baskets of grain on a wooden yoke. Although farmers were respected, their lives were often very hard. Until the late 1800s, they had to pay heavy taxes to the emperor or the local lord and were not free to leave their lord's land. They were also forbidden from wearing silk clothes, and drinking tea or *sake* (rice wine).

THRESHING

Japanese farmers are busy threshing wheat in this photograph taken in the late 1800s. Although this picture is relatively recent, the method of threshing has changed little over the centuries. The workers at the far right and the far left are separating the grains of wheat from the stalks by pulling them through wooden sieves. In the background, one worker carries a huge bundle of wheat stalks, while another stands ready with a rake and a winnowing fan. The fan was used to remove the chaff from the grain by tossing the grain in the air so that the wind blew the chaff away.

Treasures from the Sea

J APAN IS A NATION OF ISLANDS, and few people live very far from the sea. From the earliest times, Japanese people relied on the sea for food. Farms, fishing villages and huts for drying fish and seaweed were all built along Japan's rugged coastline. Heaps of oyster shells and fish bones, thrown away by the Jomon people, have survived from over 10,000 years ago.

Japanese men and women took many different kinds of food from the sea. They found crabs, shrimps and limpets in shallow water by the shore, or set sail in small boats to catch deep-sea varieties such as tuna, mackerel, shark, whale and squid. Japanese people also gathered seaweed (which contains important minerals) and other sea creatures such as jellyfish and sea-slugs. Underwater, they found treasures such as pearls and coral which were both highly prized. Specially trained divers, often women, risked their lives by holding their breath for long periods underwater to harvest these precious items. The sea also provided salt, which was collected in salt-pans (hollows built next to the sea). Salt was used to preserve fish and vegetables and to make pickles of many different kinds.

INSPIRATIONAL
Strange and beautiful sea creatures inspired Japanese painters and print-makers to create many works of art. This painting shows two flat fish and a collection of shellfish. Tuna, sea bream and salmon were all popular fish caught around the coast of Japan. They were usually grilled or preserved by salting or drying.

DANGEROUS SEAS
Japanese sailors and their boat are tossed around by wind and waves in a rough sea. This scene is depicted in a woodblock print by Utagawa Kuniyoshi. The seas around Japan's rocky coasts are often wild and stormy. Being a fisherman was, and still is, a very risky job. Late summer is the most dangerous season to go fishing because monsoon winds from the Pacific Ocean cause very violent typhoon storms. These storms can easily sink a fishing boat.

SEAFOOD

Sea products have always been very important in Japan. Oysters were collected for their pearls and also for eating. Oyster stew is still a favourite dish in southern Japan. Mussels were cooked to make many tasty dishes. They flourish in the wild, but in Japan today they are also farmed. Seaweed was used to give flavour to foods. Today it is also used as the wrapping for *maki sushi* (rolls of vinegared rice with fish and vegetable fillings).

oysters

seaweed

mussel

FISHING METHODS

For many centuries, Japanese fishermen used only baited hooks and lines. This limited the number of fish they could catch on any one trip. But after 1600 they began to use nets for fishing, which allowed them to make bigger catches.

MOTHER-OF-PEARL

Made around 1500, this domed casket is decorated with mother-of-pearl, a beautiful material that forms the coating on the inside of an oyster shell. With great skill and patience, Japanese craftworkers cut out and shaped tiny pieces of mother-of-pearl. These pieces were used to decorate many valuable items.

OYSTER COLLECTING

Gangs of oyster gatherers collect shellfish from the sea bed. Both men and women are shown working together. Oysters have thick, heavy shells, so the workers have to be fit and strong to carry full buckets back to the shore.

GATHERING SHELLFISH

Painted in the 1800s, this picture makes shellfish-gathering look like a pleasant task. In fact, hands and feet soon became numb with cold and the salt water made them red and raw.

Meals and Manners

JAPANESE FOOD has always been simple but healthy. However, for many centuries famine was a constant fear, especially among the poor. The traditional Japanese diet was based on grains – rice, millet, wheat or barley – boiled, steamed or made into noodles. Many foods were flavoured with soy sauce, made from crushed, fermented soya beans. Another nutritious soya product, *tofu* (beancurd), was made from soya beans softened and pulped in water. The pulp was formed into blocks and left to set. *Tofu* has a texture somewhere between custard and cheese, and a mild taste.

What people ate depended on who they were. Only the wealthy could afford rice, meat (usually poultry) or the finest fish. Poor families lived on what they could grow or catch for themselves.

Until the 1900s, people in Japan did not eat red meat or dairy products. But Japanese farmers grew many fruits, including pears, berries and oranges. One small, sweet orange is named after the Satsuma region in the warm southern lands of Japan.

FRESH VEGETABLES

A vegetable seller is shown here taking his produce to market. He carries it in big baskets hanging from a yoke supported on his shoulders. This photograph was taken around 1900, but the tradition of going to market every day to sell vegetables started some time around 1600. At this time many more people began to live in towns. The Japanese have always liked their food to be very fresh.

ONIGIRI - RICE BALLS

You will need: 7 cups Japanese rice, saucepan, wooden spoon, sieve, bowls, 1 tbsp salt, cutting board, 1 tbsp black sesame seeds, $^{1}/_{2}$ sheet yaki nori seaweed (optional), knife, cucumber, serving dish.

1 Ask an adult to boil the rice. Sieve to drain, but do not rinse. The rice should remain gluey. Place the rice in one bowl and the salt into another one.

2 Wet the palms of both hands with cold water. Next, put a finger into the bowl of salt and rub a little on to your palms.

3 Place one eighth of the rice on one hand. Use both hands to shape the rice into a triangle. You should use firm but not heavy pressure.

SAKE

This *sake* bottle was made almost 600 years ago, in the Bizen pottery style. *Sake* is a sweet rice wine. It was drunk by wealthy noble families and by ordinary people on very special occasions. Traditionally, it was served warm from pottery flasks or bottles such as this one and poured into tiny cups.

TEA

A servant offers a bowl of tea to a seated samurai. The Japanese believed that no matter how poor or humble people were, it was important to serve food in a gracious way. Good table manners were essential.

CHOPSTICKS

Japanese people eat using chopsticks. Traditionally, chopsticks were made from bamboo, but today many different materials, including lacquered wood, are used. In the past, rich nobles used silver chopsticks. This was mainly to display their wealth. However, they also believed the silver would help them detect any poison that had been slipped into their food. They thought that on contact with the poison, the silver would turn black.

ornate chopsticks

ordinary chopsticks

TABLEWARE

Food was served and eaten in pottery bowls and on plates. In contrast to the round and flat dishes found in many other countries, Japanese craftworkers often created tableware in elegant shapes, such as this six-sided dish.

4 Make more rice balls in the same way. Place each rice ball in one hand and sprinkle sesame seeds over the rice ball with the other.

5 If available, cut a strip of yaki nori seaweed into four and wrap some of your rice balls in it. To serve your *onigiri*, garnish them with sliced cucumber.

Rice was introduced to Japan in AD100. It has remained the staple food of the islands ever since. Serve your Japanese meal on a pretty dish and eat it with chopsticks.

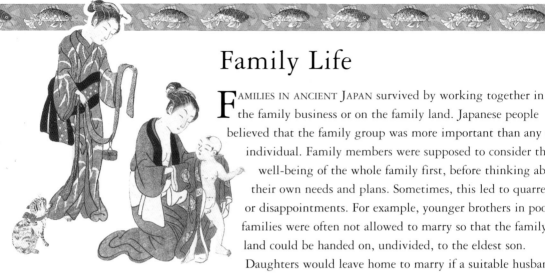

Family Life

FAMILIES IN ANCIENT JAPAN survived by working together in the family business or on the family land. Japanese people believed that the family group was more important than any one individual. Family members were supposed to consider the well-being of the whole family first, before thinking about their own needs and plans. Sometimes, this led to quarrels or disappointments. For example, younger brothers in poor families were often not allowed to marry so that the family land could be handed on, undivided, to the eldest son.

Daughters would leave home to marry if a suitable husband could be found. If not, they also remained single, in their parents' house.

Family responsibility passed down the generations, from father to eldest son. Japanese families respected age and experience because they believed it brought wisdom.

LOOKING AFTER BABY
It was women's work to care for young children. This painting shows an elegant young mother from a rich family dressing her son in a *kimono* (a robe with wide sleeves). The family maid holds the belt for the boy's *kimono*, while a pet cat watches nearby.

WORK
A little boy uses a simple machine to help winnow rice. (Winnowing separates the edible grains of rice from the outer husks.) Boys and girls from farming families were expected to help with work around the house and farmyard, and in the fields.

CARP STREAMER

You will need: pencil, 2 sheets of A1 paper, felt-tip pen, scissors, paints, paintbrush, water pot, glue, wire, masking tape, string, cane.

1 Take the pencil and one piece of paper. Draw a large carp fish shape on to the paper. When you are happy with the shape, go over it in felt-tip pen.

2 Put the second piece of paper over the first. Draw around the fish shape. Next, draw a border around the second fish and add tabs, as shown.

3 Add scales, eyes, fins and other details to both of the fishes, as shown above. Cut them both out, remembering to snip into the tabs. Paint both fishes.

PLAYTIME

These young boys have started two tops spinning close to one another. They are waiting to see what will happen when the tops touch. Japanese children had many different toys with which to play. As well as the spinning top, another great favourite was the kite.

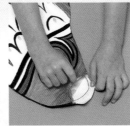

TRADITIONAL MEDICINE

Kuzu and ginger are ingredients that have been used for centuries as treatments in traditional Japanese medicine. Most traditional drugs are made from vegetables. The *kuzu* and ginger are mixed together in different ways depending on the symptoms of the patient. For example, there are 20 different mixtures for treating colds. Ginger is generally used when there is no fever.

kuzu   *ginger*

HONOURING ANCESTORS

A mother, father and child make offerings and say their prayers at a small family altar in their house. The lighted candle and paper lantern help guide the spirits to their home. Families honoured their dead ancestors at special festivals. At the festival of Obon, in summer, they greeted family spirits who had returned to earth.

4 Put the two fish shapes together, with the painted sides out. Turn the tabs in and glue the edges of the fish together, except for the tail and the mouth.

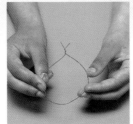

5 Use picture or garden wire to make a ring the size of the mouth. Twist the ends together, as shown Then bend them back. Bind the ends with masking tape.

6 Place the ring in the fish's mouth. Glue the ends of the mouth over the ring. Tie one end of some string on to the mouth ring and the other end to a garden cane.

Families fly carp streamers on Boy's Day (the fifth day of the fifth month) every year. One carp is flown for each son. Carp are symbols of perseverance and strength.

Houses and Homes

J APANESE BUILDERS faced many challenges when they designed homes for Japan's harsh environment. They built lightweight, single-storey houses made of straw, paper and wood. These materials would bend and sway in an earthquake. If they did collapse, or were swept away by floods, they would be less likely than a stone building to injure the people inside.

Japanese buildings were designed as a series of box-like rooms. One room was sufficient for the hut of a farming family, but a whole series of rooms could be linked together to form a royal palace. The space within was divided by screens which could be moved around to suit people's needs. Most houses had raised timber floors that were about $^1/_2$m off the ground.

LAMPS

This pottery lantern has a delicate, cut-out design and was probably for use outdoors. Inside, Japanese homes were lit by candles. A candle was placed on a stand which had four paper sides. The paper protected the candle from draughts. One side could be lifted to insert and remove the candle. There were many different styles and designs. House-fires, caused by cooking and candles, were a major hazard. They were a particular problem because so many homes were made of wood.

SILK HOUSE
For many people in Japan, home was also a place of work. Tucked under the thatched roof of this house in Eiyama, central Japan, was an attic where silk producers bred silk-worms.

MAKE A SCREEN

You will need: gold paper (44cm x 48cm), scissors, thick card (22cm x 48cm), craft knife, metal ruler, cutting board, glue stick, ruler, pencil, paints, paintbrush, water pots, fabric tape.

1 Cut two pieces of gold paper (22cm x 48cm). Use a craft knife to cut out a piece of card the same size. Stick the gold paper to both sides of the card.

2 Use a ruler and pencil to carefully mark out six equal panels, on one side of the card. Each panel should measure 22cm x 8cm.

3 Now turn your card over. Paint a traditional picture of Japanese irises, as shown above. When you have finished, leave the paint to dry.

SCREENS
Wood and paper screens were used to make both outer and inner walls. These could be pushed back to provide peaceful garden views and welcome cool breezes during Japan's hot summers.

ON THE VERANDA
Japanese buildings often had verandas (open platforms) underneath their wide, overhanging eaves. These could be used for taking fresh air, keeping lookout or enjoying a beautiful view. The people at this inn are relaxing after taking a bath in the natural hot springs.

RICH FURNISHINGS
The interior of a richly furnished building is shown in this print from 1857. Japanese furnishings were often very plain and simple. However, this house has a patterned mat and a carpet on the floor, a tall lampstand, a black and gold side table, and a brightly coloured screen dividing the room. There is also a musical instrument called a *koto* with 13 silk strings.

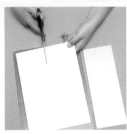

4 Turn the screen over, so the plain side is facing you. Using scissors or a craft knife, cut out each panel completely along the lines you have drawn.

5 Now use fabric tape to join each of your panels, leaving a small gap between every other panel. The tape will work as hinges for the screen.

Japanese people liked to decorate their homes with pictures of iris flowers. Traditionally, irises reminded them of absent friends.

The City in the Clouds

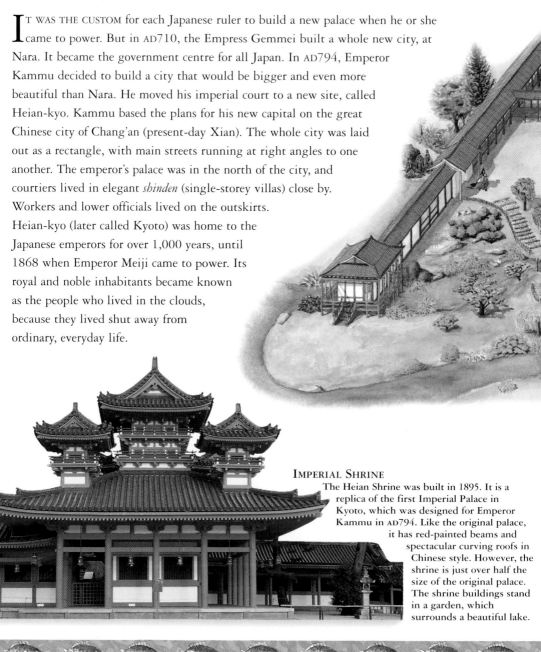

IT WAS THE CUSTOM for each Japanese ruler to build a new palace when he or she came to power. But in AD710, the Empress Gemmei built a whole new city, at Nara. It became the government centre for all Japan. In AD794, Emperor Kammu decided to build a city that would be bigger and even more beautiful than Nara. He moved his imperial court to a new site, called Heian-kyo. Kammu based the plans for his new capital on the great Chinese city of Chang'an (present-day Xian). The whole city was laid out as a rectangle, with main streets running at right angles to one another. The emperor's palace was in the north of the city, and courtiers lived in elegant *shinden* (single-storey villas) close by. Workers and lower officials lived on the outskirts. Heian-kyo (later called Kyoto) was home to the Japanese emperors for over 1,000 years, until 1868 when Emperor Meiji came to power. Its royal and noble inhabitants became known as the people who lived in the clouds, because they lived shut away from ordinary, everyday life.

IMPERIAL SHRINE

The Heian Shrine was built in 1895. It is a replica of the first Imperial Palace in Kyoto, which was designed for Emperor Kammu in AD794. Like the original palace, it has red-painted beams and spectacular curving roofs in Chinese style. However, the shrine is just over half the size of the original palace. The shrine buildings stand in a garden, which surrounds a beautiful lake.

LIFE IN A *SHINDEN*

In Heian-kyo, nobles and courtiers lived in splendid *shinden* houses like this one. Each *shinden* was designed as a number of separate buildings, linked by covered walkways. It was usually set in a landscaped garden, with artificial hills, ornamental trees, bridges, pavilions and ponds. Sometimes a stream flowed through the garden – and through parts of the house, as well. The various members of the noble family, and their servants, lived in different parts of the *shinden*.

GOLDEN PAVILION

This is a replica of the famous Kinkakuji (Temple of the Golden Pavilion). The original was completed in 1397 and survived until 1950. But, like many of Kyoto's old wooden buildings, it was destroyed by fire. The walls of the pavilion are covered in gold leaf, giving out a golden glow that is reflected in the calm waters of a shallow lake.

SILVER TEMPLE

The Ginkakuji (Temple of the Silver Pavilion) in Kyoto was completed in 1483. Despite its name, it was never painted silver, but left as natural wood.

THRONE ROOM

The Shishinden Enthronement Hall is within the palace compound in Kyoto. The emperor would have sat on the raised platform (*left*) while his courtiers bowed low before him. This palace was the main residence for all emperors from 1331 to 1868.

The Castle Builders

F OR MANY CENTURIES, powerful nobles lived in the city of Heian-kyo (later called Kyoto). But after about AD1000, some noble families began to build up large *shoen* (private estates in the countryside). These families often went to war against each other. They built castles on their lands to protect themselves, their *shoen* and the soldiers in their private armies.

Unlike all other traditional Japanese buildings (except temples), castles were several storeys high. Most were built on naturally well-defended sites such as rocky cliffs. The earliest had a *tenshu* (tall central tower) surrounded by strong wooden fences or stone walls. Later castles were more elaborate buildings, with ramparts, moats and inner and outer courtyards surrounding the central *tenshu*. The period 1570–1690 is often called the Golden Age of castle design when many magnificent castles were built by daimyo (noble warlord) families. These castles were so strong that they challenged the power of the shogun. In 1615, shogun Tokugawa Ieyasu banned noble families from building more than one castle on their estates.

CASTLE OF THE WHITE HERON
The largest surviving Japanese castle is Himeji Castle, in southern Japan. Some people say it is also the most beautiful. It is often called the Castle of the White Heron because of its graceful roofs, curved like a bird's wings. The castle was built by the Akamatsu family in the 1500s. It was taken over by warlord Toyotomi Hideyoshi in 1580.

CASTLE OF WOOD
Himeji Castle is made mostly of wood. The building work required 387 tonnes of timber and 75,000 roof tiles. Outside, strong wooden beams are covered with special fireproof plaster. Inside, there are floors and staircases of polished wood.

CASTLE UNDER SIEGE

The usual way to attack a castle was by siege. Enemy soldiers surrounded it, then waited for the inhabitants to run out of food. Meanwhile, they did all they could to break down the castle's defences by storming the gates and killing the guards.

RUN FOR IT!

This painted screen shows a siege at Osaka Castle in 1615. The inhabitants of the castle are running for their lives, chased by enemy soldiers. The castle moat and walls are visible in the background.

IN THE HEART OF THE CAPITAL

Nijo Castle, Kyoto, was begun by warrior Oda Nobunaga in 1569, and finished by Tokugawa Ieyasu. It was designed to give its owner total control over the emperor's capital city – and all Japan.

BUILDING MATERIALS

Castles were built of wood such as pine and stone. For the lower walls, huge boulders were cut roughly from the quarries or collected from mountainsides. They were fitted together by hand without mortar so that in an earthquake the boulders could move slightly without the whole building collapsing. Castle stonework was usually left rough, but it was occasionally chiselled to a fine, smooth finish. Upper walls were made of wooden planks and spars, covered with plaster made from crushed stone mixed with water.

pine   limestone

SURROUNDED BY WATER

Castles were surrounded by wide, deep moats to keep out invaders. A typical moat might be 20m wide and 6m deep. The only way into the castle was across a wooden drawbridge guarded by soldiers at both ends. The castle was also defended by strong stone ramparts, often 5m thick. They sloped into the moat so that any attacker could easily be seen from above.

Towns and Trade

Until modern times (after around 1900) most Japanese people lived in the countryside. But after 1600, when Japan was at peace, castle-towns in particular grew rapidly. Towns and cities were great centres of craftwork and trade. As one visitor to Kyoto commented in 1691, 'There is hardly a household... where there is not something made or sold.' Trade also increased in small towns and villages, linking even the most remote districts into a countrywide network of buying and selling.

Castle-towns were carefully planned. Roads, gates, walls and water supplies were laid out in an orderly design. Areas of the town were set aside for different groups of people to live and work – nobles, daimyo and high-ranking samurai families, ordinary samurai, craftworkers, merchants and traders. Many towns became centres of entertainment with theatres, puppet plays, dancers, musicians and artists. Big cities also had pleasure districts where the inhabitants could escape from the pressures of everyday life.

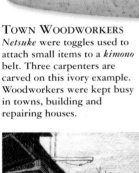

Town Woodworkers
Netsuke were toggles used to attach small items to a *kimono* belt. Three carpenters are carved on this ivory example. Woodworkers were kept busy in towns, building and repairing houses.

A Traditional Town
This picture was drawn by a visiting European artist in 1882. It shows a narrow, busy street in a Japanese city. Although it is a relatively recent picture, it shows styles of clothes, shops and houses that had existed for several hundred years. The buildings are made of wood and the shops open directly on to the streets. The cloth hangings above the doorways represent the type of shop, for example, knife shop or fan shop. They are printed or woven with *kanji* characters or special designs. The European artist obviously could not read Japanese because the writing on the shop boards and banners is meaningless squiggles.

MANY DIFFERENT CRAFTS

These two men are busy making paper lanterns. From the earliest times craftworkers with many different skills worked in Japanese towns. One list of craft guilds, drawn up in Osaka in 1784, included 24 trades. They ranged from makers of porcelain, parasols and face-powder, to basket-weavers, printers, paper-sellers, paint-mixers, cotton-spinners, ivory carvers, and makers of socks.

SKILLED AT WEAVING SILK

Silk was woven on a loom like the one shown here. This woodblock print dates from about 1770. Towns were great centres of cloth production. Kyoto, in particular, was famous for its silk fabrics patterned with gold and silver flowers.

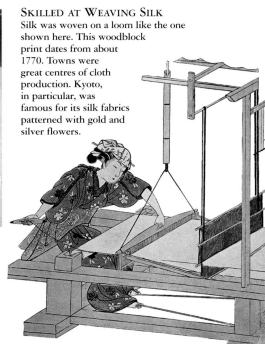

PLEASURE PURSUIT

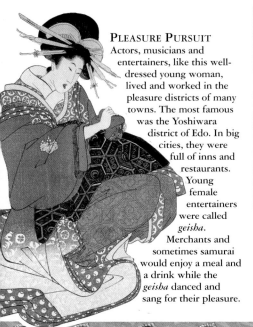

Actors, musicians and entertainers, like this well-dressed young woman, lived and worked in the pleasure districts of many towns. The most famous was the Yoshiwara district of Edo. In big cities, they were full of inns and restaurants. Young female entertainers were called *geisha*. Merchants and sometimes samurai would enjoy a meal and a drink while the *geisha* danced and sang for their pleasure.

FIRE HAZARD

Fire was a constant danger in Japanese cities. This was because most buildings were made of wood and packed close together. In an effort to prevent fires from spreading, city rulers gave orders that wooden roof-coverings should be replaced by fireproof clay tiles. They also decreed that tubs of water should be placed in city streets, and watch-towers built to give advance warning of fire.

Palace Fashions

IN ANCIENT JAPAN, rich noble men and women at the emperor's court wore very different clothes from ordinary peasant farmers. From around AD600 to 1500, Japanese court fashions were based on traditional Chinese styles. Both men and women wore long, flowing robes made of many layers of fine, glossy silk, held in place by a sash and cords. Men also wore wide trousers underneath. Women kept their hair loose and long, whilst men tied their hair into a topknot and wore a tall black hat. Elegance and refinement were the aims of this style.

After about 1500, wealthy samurai families began to choose new styles. Men and women wore *kimono* – long, loose robes. *Kimono* also became popular among wealthy artists, actors and craftworkers. The shoguns passed laws to try to stop ordinary people from wearing elaborate *kimono*, but they proved impossible to enforce.

PARASOL
Women protected their delicate complexions with sunshades made of oiled paper. The fashion was for pale skin, often heavily powdered, with dark, soft eyebrows.

GOOD TASTE OR GAUDY?
This woman's outfit dates from the 1700s. Though striking, it would probably have been considered too bold to be in the most refined taste. Men and women took great care in choosing garments that blended well together.

MAKE A FAN

You will need: thick card (38cm x 26cm), pencil, ruler, compasses, protractor, felt tip pen (blue), paper (red), scissors, paints, paintbrush, water pot, glue stick.

1 Draw a line down the centre of the piece of card. Place your compasses two-thirds of the way up the line. Draw a circle 23cm in diameter.

2 Add squared-off edges at the top of the circle, as shown. Now draw your handle (15cm long). The handle should be directly over the vertical line.

3 Place a protractor at the top of the handle and draw a semicircle around it. Now mark lines every 2.5 degrees. Draw pencil lines through these marks.

FEET OFF THE GROUND
To catch insects in a garden by lamplight these women are wearing *geta* (clogs). *Geta* were designed to protect the wearer's feet from mud and rain by raising them about 5–7cm above the ground. They were worn outdoors.

SILK *KIMONO*
This beautiful silk *kimono* was made in about 1600. Women wore a wide silk sash called an *obi* on top of their *kimono*. Men fastened their *kimono* with a narrow sash.

PAPER FAN
Folding fans, made of pleated paper, were a Japanese invention. They were carried by both men and women. This one is painted with gold leaf and chrysanthemum flowers.

BEAUTIFUL HAIR
Traditional palace fashions for men and women are shown in this scene from the imperial palace. The women have long, flowing hair that reaches to their waists – a sign of great beauty in early Japan.

It was the custom for Japanese noblewomen to hide their faces in court. They used decorated fans such as this one as a screen. Fans were also used to help people keep cool on hot, humid summer days.

4 Draw a blue line 1cm to the left of each line you have drawn. Then draw a blue line 2mm to the right of this line. Add a squiggle between sections.

5 Cut out your card fan. Now use this as a template. Draw around the fan top (not handle) on to your red paper. Cut out the red paper.

6 Now cut out the in-between sections on your card fan (those marked with a squiggle). Paint the card fan brown on both sides. Leave to dry.

7 Paint the red paper with white flowers and leave to dry. Paste glue on to one side of the card fan. Stick the undecorated side of the red paper to the fan.

Working Clothes

O RDINARY PEOPLE IN JAPAN could not afford the rich, silk robes worn by emperors, nobles and samurai families. Instead, they wore plain, simple clothes that gave them freedom to move easily as they went about their daily tasks. Men wore baggy jackets and loose trousers, whilst women wore simple, long wrap-over robes.

Ordinary clothes were made from rough, inexpensive fibres, woven at home or purchased in towns. Cotton, hemp and ramie (a plant rather like flax) were all popular. Many other plants were also used to make cloth, including plantain (banana) and the bark of the mulberry tree. From around 1600, clothes were dyed with indigo (a blue dye) and were sometimes woven in complicated *ikat* patterns.

Japan's climate varies from cold and snowy in winter to hot and steamy in summer, so working peoples' clothes had to be adaptable. Usually people added or removed layers of clothing depending on the season. To cope with the rainy summers, they made waterproof clothes from straw. In winter, they wore padded or quilted jackets.

PROTECTIVE APRONS
These women are making salt from sea water. They are wearing aprons made out of leather or heavy canvas cloth to protect their clothes. The woman on the right has tied back her long hair with a scarf.

LOOSE AND COMFY
Farmworkers are shown hard at work planting rice seedlings in a flooded paddy-field. They are wearing loose, comfortable clothes – short jackets, baggy trousers tied at the knee and ankle, and shady hats. For working in water, in rice-fields or by the seashore, ordinary men and women often went barefoot.

MAKE DO AND MEND

Working clothes often got frayed or torn and it was a woman's job to mend them with needle and thread.
Women in poor, ordinary families usually made rough, simple clothes for their own families. Sometimes they also bought clothes from travelling pedlars or small shops.

ARMOURERS AT WORK

Loose, flowing *kimono* were originally worn only by high-ranking families. Before long other wealthy and prestigious people, such as these skilled armour makers, copied them. *Kimono* were elegant and comfortable. However, they were certainly not suitable for active outdoor work.

FITTING FOOTWEAR

Out of doors, ordinary people wore clogs or simple sandals. The sandals were woven from straw and held on by twisted straw strings. Before entering a house, people always took off their outdoor footwear so as not to bring mud, grass and dirt inside.

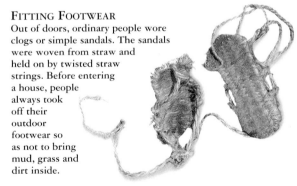

KEEPING THE RAIN OUT

Cone-shaped hats made of woven straw or bamboo protected people's heads from rain. The sloping shape of these hats helped the rainwater to run off before it had time to soak in. Farmworkers also made rain-capes out of straw matting. In this picture you can see one man bent almost double under his rain-cape (*right*). To protect themselves from the rain, rich people used umbrellas made of oiled cloth.

The Decorative Arts

THERE IS A LONG TRADITION among Japanese craftworkers of making everyday things as beautiful as possible. Craftworkers also created exquisite items for the wealthiest and most knowledgeable collectors. They used a wide variety of materials – pottery, metal, lacquer, cloth, paper and bamboo. Pottery ranged from plain, simple earthenware to delicate porcelain, painted with brilliantly coloured glazes. Japanese metalworkers produced alloys (mixtures of metals) that were unknown elsewhere in the ancient world. Cloth was woven from many fibres in elaborate designs. Bamboo and other plants from the grass family were woven into elegant *tatami* mats (floor mats) and containers of all different shapes and sizes. Japanese craftworkers also made beautifully decorated *inro* (little boxes, used like purses) which dangled from men's *kimono* sashes.

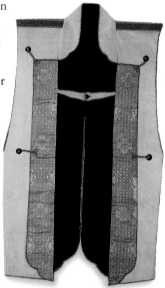

SHINY LACQUER
This samurai helmet was made for ceremonial use. It is covered in lacquer (varnish) and decorated with a diving dolphin. Producing shiny lacquerware was a slow process. An object was covered with many thin layers of lacquer. Each layer was allowed to dry, then polished, before more lacquer was applied. The lacquer could then be carved.

SAMURAI SURCOAT
Even the simplest garments were beautifully crafted. This surcoat (loose, sleeveless tunic) was made for a member of the noble Mori family, probably around 1800. Surcoats were worn by samurai on top of their armour.

MAKE A *NETSUKE* FOX

You will need: paper, pencil, ruler, self-drying clay, balsa wood, modelling tool, fine sandpaper, acrylic paint, paintbrush, water pot, darning needle, cord, small box (for an inro*), scissors, toggle, wide belt.*

1 Draw a square 5cm by 5cm on a piece of paper. Roll out a ball of clay to the size of the square. Shape the clay so that it comes to a point at one end.

2 Turn your clay over. Lay a stick of balsa approximately 6cm long, along the back. Stick a thin sausage of clay over the stick. Press to secure.

3 Turn the clay over. Cut out two triangles of clay. Join them to the head using the tool. Make indentations to shape them into a fox's ears.

METALWORK

Craftworkers polish the sharp swords and knives they have made. It took many years of training to become a metalworker. Japanese craftsmen were famous for their fine skills at smelting and handling metals.

BOXES FOR BELTS

Inro were originally designed for storing medicines. The first *inro* were plain and simple, but after about 1700 they were often decorated with exquisite designs. These *inro* have been lacquered (coated with a shiny substance made from the sap of the lacquer tree). Inside, they contain several compartments stacked on top of each other.

MASTERWORK

This beautiful jar is decorated with a design of white flowers, painted over a shiny red and black glaze. It was painted by the master-craftsman Ogata Kenzan, who lived from 1663 to 1743.

Wear your inro *dangling from your belt. In ancient Japan,* inro *were usually worn by men. They were held in place with carved toggles called* netsuke.

4 Use the handle of your modelling tool to make your fox's mouth. Carve eyes, nostrils, teeth and a frown line. Use the top of a pencil to make eye holes.

5 Leave to dry. Gently sand the *netsuke* and remove the balsa wood stick. Paint it with several layers of acrylic paint. Leave in a warm place to dry.

6 Thread cord through the four corners of a small box with a darning needle. Then thread the cord through a toggle and the *netsuke,* as shown.

7 Put a wide belt round your waist. Thread the *netsuke* under the belt. It should rest on the top of it. The *inro* (box) should hang down, as shown.

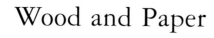

Wood and Paper

IN ANCIENT JAPAN, woodworking was an art as well as a craft. Most large Japanese buildings, such as temples and palaces, were decorated with elaborately carved, painted and gilded wooden roofs. Doorways and pillars were also painted or carved. Inside, ceiling-beams and supporting pillars were made from strong tree trunks, floors were laid with polished wooden strips, and sliding screens had finely made wooden frames. A display of woodworking skill in a building demonstrated the owner's wealth and power. However, some smaller wooden buildings were left deliberately plain, allowing the quality of the materials and craftsmanship, and the elegance of the design, to speak for themselves.

Paper was another very important Japanese craft. It was used to make many fine objects – from wall-screens to lanterns, sunshades and even clothes. The choice of the best paper for writing a poem or painting a picture was part of an artist's task. Fine paper also showed off a letter-writer's elegance and good taste.

WOODEN STATUES
This statue portrays a Buddhist god. It was carved between AD800 and 900. Many Japanese temples contain carvings and statues made from wood.

SCREENS WITH SCENES
Screens were movable works of art. This example, made in the 1700s, portrays a scene from Japanese history. It shows Portuguese merchants and missionaries listening to Japanese musicians.

ORIGAMI BOX
You will need: a square of origami paper (15cm x 15cm), clean and even folding surface.

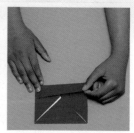

1 Place your paper on a flat surface. Fold it horizontally across the centre. Next fold it vertically across the centre and unfold.

2 Carefully fold each corner to the centre point as shown. Unfold each corner crease before starting to make the next one.

3 Using the creases, fold all the corners back into the centre. Now fold each side 2cm from the edge to make a crease and then unfold.

GRAND PILLARS

This row of red wooden pillars supports a heavy, ornate roof. It is part of the Meiji Shrine in Tokyo. Red (or cinnabar) was the traditional Japanese colour for shrines and royal palaces.

HOLY LIGHTS

Lamps made of pleated paper were often hung outside Shinto shrines. They were painted with the names of people who had donated money to the shrines.

PAPER ART

Paper-making and calligraphy (beautiful writing) were two very important art forms in Japan. This woodcut shows a group of people with everything they need to decorate scrolls and fans— paper, ink, palette, calligraphy brushes and pots of paint.

USEFUL AND BEAUTIFUL

Trees were admired for their beauty as well as their usefulness. These spring trees were portrayed by the famous Japanese woodblock printer, Hiroshige.

Japanese people used boxes of all shapes and sizes to store their possessions. What will you keep in your box?

4 Carefully unfold two opposite side panels. Your origami box should now look like the structure shown in the picture above.

5 Following the crease marks you have already made, turn in the side panels to make walls, as shown in the picture. Turn the origami round 90°.

6 Use your fingers to push the corners of the third side in, as shown. Use the existing crease lines as a guide. Raise the box slightly and fold the wall over.

7 Next, carefully repeat step 6 to construct the final wall. You could try making another origami box to perfect your technique.

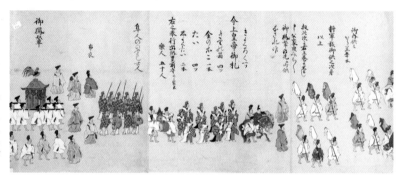

printed kanji → katakana		printed kanji → handwritten kanji → hiragana		
阿	ア	以 →	→	い
伊	イ	呂 →	→	ろ
宇	ウ	波 →	→	は
江	エ	仁 →	→	に
於	オ	保 →	→	ほ

Writing and Drawing

THE JAPANESE LANGUAGE belongs to a family of languages that includes Finnish, Turkish and Korean. It is totally different from its neighbouring language, Chinese. Yet, for many centuries, Chinese characters were used for reading and writing Japanese. This was because people such as monks, courtiers and the emperor – the only people who could read and write – valued Chinese civilization and ideas.

As the Japanese kingdom grew stronger, and Japanese culture developed, it became clear that a new way of writing Japanese was required. Around AD800, two new *kana* (ways of writing) were invented. Both used picture-symbols developed from *kanji* (Chinese characters) that expressed sounds and were written using a brush and ink on scrolls of paper. One type, called *hiragana*, was used for purely Japanese words; the other, called *katakana*, was used for words from elsewhere.

JAPANESE WRITING

Around AD800 two new writing systems, *hiragana* and *katakana,* were invented. For the first time, people could write Japanese exactly as they spoke it. The left-hand side of the chart above shows how a selection of *katakana* symbols developed from the original *kanji*. The right-hand side of the chart shows how *hiragana* symbols evolved, via the handwritten form of *kanji*.

OFFICIAL RECORDS

This illustrated scroll records the visit of Emperor Go-Mizunoo (ruled 1611–1629) to Shogun Tokugawa Iemitsu. The writing tells us that the palanquin (litter) in the picture carries the empress and gives a list of presents for the shogun.

CALLIGRAPHY

You will need: paper, ink, a calligraphy brush. (Please note that you can use an ordinary paint brush and black paint if you cannot find a calligraphy brush or any ink.)

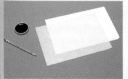

The numbers show the order of the strokes required for this character. Strokes 2, 3 & 4, and 5 & 6, are written in one movement, without lifting the brush.

1 The first stroke is called *soku*. Begin near the top of the paper, going from left to right. Move the brush sharply towards the bottom left, then lift it off the paper.

2 Strokes 2, 3 and 4 are called *roku, do* and *yaku*. Write them together in one movement. Apply pressure as you begin each stroke and then release again.

STORIES ON SCROLLS

Scrolls such as this one were designed to be hand-held, like a book. Words and pictures are side-by-side. Japanese artists often painted buildings with the roofs off, so that readers could see inside.

PAINTING PICTURES

A young boy is shown here mixing ink for his female companion. The ink is made from compressed charcoal that is dissolved in water to give the ink the required consistency. The artist herself has selected a broad brush to begin her painting.

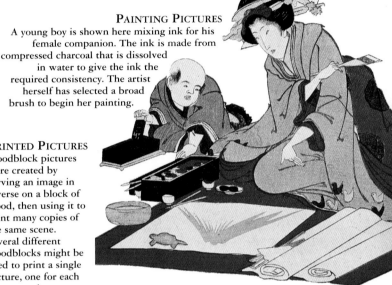

PRINTED PICTURES

Woodblock pictures were created by carving an image in reverse on a block of wood, then using it to print many copies of the same scene. Several different woodblocks might be used to print a single picture, one for each separate colour.

3 For stroke 5 (*saku*) apply an even amount of pressure as you draw your brush left to right. For 6 (*ryo*), apply pressure at the beginning and release it.

4 Stroke 7 is called *taku*. Apply even pressure overall to make this short stroke. Make sure that you also make the stroke quite quickly.

5 Stroke 8 is also called *taku*. Apply an increasing amount of pressure as the brush travels down. Turn the brush back to the right at the last moment, as shown.

This character is called EI (eternal). It uses all eight major Japanese calligraphy strokes.

45

Poems, Letters and Novels

NEW WAYS OF WRITING the Japanese language were invented around AD800. This led to the growth of forms of literature such as diaries, travel writing and poems. Elegant, refined poetry (called *waka*) was very popular at the emperor's court. From about 1600, *haiku* (short poems with 17 syllables) became the favourite form. *Haiku* were written by people from the samurai class, as well as by courtiers.

Women prose writers were especially important in early Japan. The courtier, Sei Shonagon (born around AD965) won praise for her *Pillow Book* – a kind of diary. Women writers were so famous that at least one man pretended to be a woman. The male poet Ki no Tsurayuki wrote *The Tosa Diary* under a woman's name.

LITERARY LADY
Lady Chiyo was a courtier and poet in the 1700s. Nobles read and wrote a lot of poetry. It was considered a sign of good breeding to quote from literary works. Letters to and from nobles often contained lines from poems.

THE WORLD'S FIRST NOVEL
This scroll shows a scene from the *Tale of Genji*, written in about AD1000 by Lady Murasaki Shikibu. The scroll was painted in the 1700s, but the artist has used a painting style from the period in which the story was written.

MAKE PAPER

You will need: 8 pieces of wood (4 x 33cm and 4 x 28cm), nails, hammer, muslin (35cm x 30cm), staple gun, electrical tape, scissors, torn-up paper, water bowl, masher, washing-up bowl, flower petals, spoon, soft cloths.

1 Ask an adult to make two frames. Staple stretched muslin on to one frame. Cover this frame with electrical tape to make the screen, as shown.

2 Put the frame and screen to one side. Soak paper scraps overnight in water. Mash into a pulp with the potato masher. It should look like porridge.

3 Half-fill the washing-up bowl with the pulp and cold water. You could add a few flower petals for decoration. Mix well with a spoon.

46

JAPANESE PAPER

Japanese craftworkers made many different kinds of beautiful paper. They used tree bark (especially the bark of the mulberry tree) or other plant fibres, which they blended carefully to create different thicknesses and textures of paper. They sometimes sprinkled the paper mixture with mica or gold leaf to produce rich, sparkling effects.

Japanese paper

mulberry bark

CRANES ON A CARD

This poem-card contains a traditional *waka* (palace-style) poem, in 31 syllables. It is written in silver and black and decorated with cranes.

POET AND TRAVELLER

The poet Matsuo Basho (1644-1694) is portrayed in this print dating from the 1800s. Basho was famous as a writer of short *haiku* poems. He was also a great traveller, and in this picture he is shown (*right*) talking to two farmers he has met on his travels. Here is a typical example of a *haiku* by Basho:

> The summer grasses –
> All that has survived from
> Brave warriors' dreams.

The personality of a Japanese writer was judged by the type of paper they used, as well as by the content of the letter.

4 Place the screen with the frame on top into the washing up bowl. As the frame and screen enter the water, scoop under the pulpy mixture.

5 Pull the screen out of the pulp, keeping it level. Gently move it from side to side over the bowl to allow a layer of pulp to form. Shake the water off.

6 Take the frame off the screen. Carefully lay the screen face down on a cloth. Mop the back of the screen with a cloth to get rid of the excess water.

7 Peel away the screen. Leave the paper to dry for at least 6 hours. When dry, turn over and gently peel away the cloth to reveal your paper.

At the Theatre

GOING TO THE THEATRE and listening to music were popular pastimes in ancient Japan. There were several kinds of Japanese drama. They developed from religious dances at temples and shrines, or from slow, stately dances performed at the emperor's court.

Noh is the oldest form of Japanese drama. It developed in the 1300s from rituals and dances that had been performed for centuries before. Noh plays were serious and dignified. The actors performed on a bare stage, with only a backdrop. They chanted or sang their words, accompanied by drums and a flute. Noh performances were traditionally held in the open air, often at a shrine.

Kabuki plays were first seen around 1600. In 1629, the shoguns banned women performers and so male actors took their places. Kabuki plays became very popular in the new, fast-growing towns.

GRACEFUL PLAYER
This woman entertainer is holding a *shamisen* – a three-stringed instrument, played by plucking the strings. The *shamisen* often formed part of a group, together with a *koto* (zither) and flute.

POPULAR PUPPETS
Bunraku (puppet plays) originated about 400 years ago, when *shamisen* music, dramatic chanting and hand-held puppets were combined. The puppets were so large and complex that it took three men to move them about on stage.

NOH THEATRE MASK

You will need: tape measure, balloon, newspaper, bowl, glue, petroleum jelly, pin, scissors, felt-tip pen, modelling clay, bradawl, paints (red, yellow, black, and white), paintbrush, water pot, cord.

1 Ask a friend to measure around your head above the ears. Blow up a balloon to fit this measurement. This will be the base for the papier-mâché.

2 Rip up strips of newspaper. Soak in a water and glue mixture (1 part glue to 2 parts water). Cover the balloon with a layer of petroleum jelly.

3 Cover the front and sides of your balloon with a layer of papier-mâché. Leave to dry. Repeat 2 or 3 times. When dry, pop the balloon.

TRAGIC
THEATRE
An audience
watches a scene
from an outdoor
performance of a
Noh play. Noh
drama was
always about
important and
serious topics.
Favourite subjects
were death and
the afterlife,
and the plays
were often
very tragic.

LOUD AND FAST
Kabuki plays were a complete contrast to
Noh. They were fast-moving, loud, flashy
and very dramatic. Audiences admired the
skills of the actors as much as the
cleverness or thoughtfulness of the plots.

BEHIND THE MASK
This Noh mask represents a warrior's face.
Noh drama did not try to be lifelike. The actors all
wore masks and moved very slowly using stiff,
stylized gestures to express their feelings.
Noh plays were all performed by men. Actors playing
women's parts wore female clothes and masks.

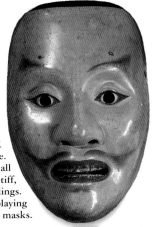

*Put on your mask and feel like
an actor in an ancient
Noh play. Imagine
that you are
wearing his
long, swirling
robes, too.*

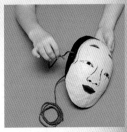

4 Trim the papier-mâché
so that it forms a mask
shape. Ask a friend to
mark where your eyes,
nose and mouth are when
you hold it to your face.

5 Cut out the face holes
with scissors. Put clay
beneath the side of the
mask at eye level. Use a
bradawl to make two holes
on each side.

6 Paint the face of a calm
young lady from Noh
theatre on your mask. Use
this picture as your guide.
The mask would have
been worn by a man.

7 Fit the cord through
the holes at each side.
Tie one end. Once you
have adjusted the mask
so that it fits, tie the
other end.

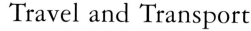

Travel and Transport

J APAN IS A RUGGED and mountainous country. Until the 20th century, the only way to travel through its wild countryside was along narrow, zig-zag paths. These mountain paths and fragile wooden bridges across deep gullies and rushing streams were often swept away by landslides or floods.

During the Heian period, wealthy warriors rode fine horses, while important officials, wealthy women, children and priests travelled in lightweight wood and bamboo carts. These carts were fitted with screens and curtains for privacy and were pulled by oxen. In places where the route was unsuitable for ox-carts, wealthy people were carried shoulder-high on palanquins (lightweight portable boxes or litters). Ordinary people mostly travelled on foot.

During the Tokugawa period (1600–1868) the shoguns encouraged new road building as a way of increasing trade and control. The longest road was the Eastern Sea Road, which ran for 480km between Kyoto and the shogun's capital, Edo. Some people said it was the busiest road in the world.

BEASTS OF BURDEN
A weary mother rests with her child and ox during their journey. You can see that the ox is loaded up with heavy bundles. Ordinary people could not afford horses, so they used oxen to carry heavy loads or to pull carts.

SHOULDER HIGH
Noblewomen on palanquins (litters) are shown being taken by porters across a deep river. Some of the women have decided to disembark so that they can be carried across the river. Palanquins were used in Japan right up to the Tokugawa period (1600–1868). When making journeys to or from the city of Edo, daimyo and wives were sometimes carried the whole route in palanquins.

Hugging the Coastline

Ships sail into harbour at Tempozan, Osaka. Cargo between Edo and Osaka was mostly carried by ships that hugged the coastline. The marks on the sails show the company that owned the ships.

Carrying Cargo

Little cargo-boats, such as these at Edobashi in Edo, carried goods along rivers or around the coast. They were driven through the water by men rowing with oars or pushing against the river bed with a long pole.

Steep Mountain Paths

Travellers on mountain paths hoped to find shelter for the night in villages, temples or monasteries. It could take all day to walk 16km along rough mountain tracks.

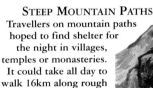

In the Harbour

Sea-going sailing ships, laden with cargo, are shown here at anchor in the harbour of Osaka (an important port in south-central Japan). In front of them you can see smaller river-boats with tall sails. Some families both lived and worked on river-boats.

Remote from the World

Japan's geographical position has always kept it separate from the rest of the world, but this has not meant total isolation. The Japanese have established links with their nearest neighbours and, sometimes, with lands far away.

In AD588 the first Buddhist temple was built in Japan. Its construction marked the beginning of an era when Chinese religious beliefs, styles in art, clothes and painting, and beliefs about government and society, began to play an important part in Japan. This Chinese-style era ended between AD800 and 900. By that time, Japanese culture had grown strong and confident.

The next important contact with foreigners came when European traders and missionaries arrived in Japan in the 1540s. At first they were tolerated but, between 1635 and 1640, the shoguns banned Christianity altogether and strictly limited the places where foreigners could trade. Europeans had to live within the Dutch trading factory (trading post) on Dejima Island. Chinese merchants were allowed in only a few streets in Nagasaki. This policy of isolationism continued until 1853, when the USA sent gunboats and demands to trade. Reluctantly, the Japanese agreed and, in 1858, they signed a treaty of friendship with America.

KONG FUZI
The Chinese thinker and teacher Kong Fuzi (often known as Confucius) lived from 551 to 479BC. His ideas about family life, government and society influenced many later generations in both China and Korea. Chinese scribes took Kong Fuzi's ideas to Japan in about AD552.

IN WESTERN STYLE
The young Emperor Meiji took over from the shoguns in 1868. In this picture, leading members of his government meet to discuss foreign policy in 1877. Most of them are wearing Western-style army and navy uniforms.

52

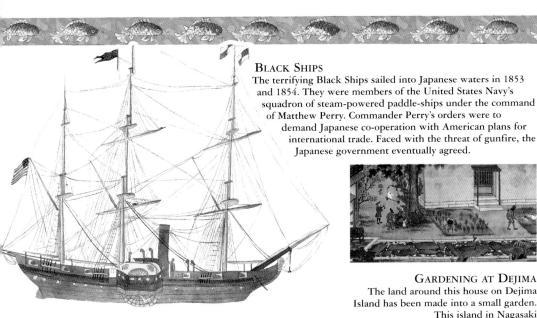

BLACK SHIPS
The terrifying Black Ships sailed into Japanese waters in 1853 and 1854. They were members of the United States Navy's squadron of steam-powered paddle-ships under the command of Matthew Perry. Commander Perry's orders were to demand Japanese co-operation with American plans for international trade. Faced with the threat of gunfire, the Japanese government eventually agreed.

GARDENING AT DEJIMA
The land around this house on Dejima Island has been made into a small garden. This island in Nagasaki harbour was the only area where Europeans were allowed to stay during Japan's period of isolation from the world.

BUSINESS IN DEJIMA
This painting from the 1700s portrays European and Japanese merchants and their servants at the Dutch trading factory at Dejima. The artist has shown the merchants discussing business and taking tea in a Japanese-style house furnished with some European-style contents.

IDEAS FROM ABROAD
An American-style steam train travels across Yokohama harbour. This print is from the Meiji era (1868 onwards), the period when Western-style ideas were introduced by the emperor. In the background you can see Yokohama docks which became a major centre of new industries in the late 1800s.

Gods and Spirits

ALMOST ALL OF THE Japanese people followed a very ancient religious faith called Shinto. Shinto means the way of the gods. It developed from a central idea that all natural things had a spiritual side. These natural spirits – called *kami* in Japanese – were often kindly, but could be powerful or even dangerous. They needed to be respected and worshipped. Shinto also encouraged ancestor-worship – ancestor spirits could guide, help and warn. Special priests, called shamans, made contact with all these spirits by chanting, fasting, or by falling into a trance.

Shinto spirits were honoured at shrines that were often built close to sites of beauty or power, such as waterfalls or volcanoes. Priests guarded the purity of each shrine, and held rituals to make offerings to the spirits. Each Shinto shrine was entered through a *torii* (large gateway) which marked the start of the sacred space. *Torii* always had the same design – they were based on the ancient perches of birds waiting to be sacrificed.

AT THE SHRINE
A priest worships by striking a drum at the Grand Shrine at Izu, one of the oldest Shinto shrines in Japan. A festival is held there every August, with processions, offerings and prayers. An *omikoshi* (portable shrine) is carried through the streets, so that the spirits can bring blessings to everyone.

OFFERINGS TO THE SPIRITS
Worshippers at Shinto shrines leave offerings for the *kami* (spirits) that live there. These offerings are neatly-wrapped barrels of *sake* (rice wine). Today, worshippers also leave little wooden plaques with prayers on them.

VOTIVE DOLLS
You will need: self-drying clay, 2 balsa wood sticks (12cm long), ruler, paints, paintbrush, water pot, modelling clay, silver foil, red paper, gold paper, scissors, pencil, glue stick, optional basket and dowelling stick.

1 Place a ball of clay on the end of each of the balsa sticks. On one of the sticks, push the clay down so that it is 5mm from the end. This will be the man.

2 Paint hair and features on the man. Stand it up in modelling clay to dry. Repeat with the woman. Cover the 5mm excess stick on the man's head in foil.

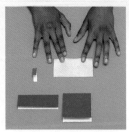

3 Take two pieces of red paper, 6.5cm x 14cm and 6cm x 10cm. Fold them in half. Take two pieces of gold paper, 10.5cm x 10cm and 1cm x 7cm. Fold in half.

LUCKY GOD

Daikoku is one of seven lucky gods from India, China and Japan that are associated with good fortune. In Japan, he is the special god of farmers, wealth, and of the kitchen. Daikoku is recognized by both Shinto and Buddhist religions.

HOLY VOLCANO

Fuji-San (Mount Fuji) has been honoured as a holy place since the first people arrived in Japan. Until 1867, women were not allowed to set foot on Fuji's holy ground.

FLOATING GATE

This *torii* at Miyajima (Island of Shrines), in southern Japan, is built on the seashore. It appears to float on the water as the tide flows in. Miyajima was sacred to the three daughters of the Sun.

In some regions of Japan, dolls like these are put on display in baskets every year at Hinamatsuri (Girls' Day), on 3 March.

4 Take the folded red paper (6.5cm x 14cm). This is the man's *kimono*. Cut a triangular shape out of the bottom. Cut a neck hole out at the folded end.

5 Dip the blunt end of the pencil in white paint. Stipple a pattern on to the red paper. Add the central dots using the pencil tip dipped in paint.

6 Slip the man's head and body into the red paper *kimono*. Then take the larger piece of gold paper and fold around the stick, as shown. Glue in place.

7 Now stick the gold paper (1cm x 7cm) on to the woman's *kimono*, in the middle. Slip the woman's head and body into the *kimono*. Glue in place.

Monks and Priests

AS WELL AS FOLLOWING SHINTO, many Japanese people also practised the Buddhist faith. Prince Siddhartha Gautama, the founder of Buddhism, was born in Nepal around 500BC. He left his home to teach a new religion based on the search for truth and harmony and the ending of all selfish desires. His followers called him the Buddha (the enlightened one). The most devoted Buddhists spent at least part of their life as scholars, priests, monks or nuns.

Buddhist teachings first reached Japan in AD552, brought by monks and scribes from China and Korea. Buddhism encouraged learning and scholarship, and, over the centuries, many different interpretations of the Buddha's teachings developed. Each was taught by dedicated monks or priests and attracted many followers. The Buddhist monk Shinran (1173–1262) urged his followers to place their faith in Amida Buddha (a calm, kindly form of the Buddha). He taught them that Amida Buddha would lead them after death to the Western Paradise. Shinran's rival, Nichiren (1222–1282) claimed that he had been divinely chosen to spread the True Word. This was Nichiren's own interpretation of Buddhism, based on an ancient Buddhist text called the *Lotus Sutra*.

MONK AND PUPIL
A Buddhist sage is pictured with one of his pupils. Thanks to such teachers, Buddhist ideas spread beyond the imperial court to reach ordinary people, and many Buddhist temples and monasteries were built.

FAMOUS MONK
This woodcut of 1857 shows an episode from a story about the Buddhist monk, Nichiren. He was said to have calmed a storm by the power of his prayers. The influence of Nichiren continued long after his death, and many other stories were told about him.

SCHOLAR MONKS

A group of monks (*left*) study Buddhist scrolls. Monks were among the most important scholars in early Japan. They studied ancient Chinese knowledge and developed new Japanese ideas.

GREAT BUDDHA

This huge bronze statue of Daibutsu (the Great Buddha) is 11.3m high and weighs 93 tonnes. It was made at Kamakura in 1252 – a time when the city was rich and powerful. The statue shows the Buddha in Amida form – inviting worshippers to the Western Paradise.

GOD OF MERCY

Standing over 5m high, this statue of Kannon was made around AD700. Kannon is also known as the god of mercy. Orginally Kannon was a man – in fact, one form of the Buddha himself. However, over the years it became the custom to portray him in female shape.

HOLY FLOWERS

The lotus flower often grows in dirty water and was believed to symbolize the purity of a holy life. It has many associations in literature with Buddhism. Chrysanthemums are often placed on graves or on Buddhist altars in the home. White and yellow flowers are most popular because these colours are associated with death.

white chrysanthemum

yellow chrysanthemums

lotus

HOLY WORDS

For many years after Buddhism reached Japan, it was practised mainly by educated, wealthy people. Only they could read the beautiful Buddhist *sutras* (religious texts) like this one, created between AD645 and 794. This sutra was written by hand, but some of the world's first printed documents are Buddhist *sutras* made in Japan.

Temples and Gardens

Land suitable for growing plants was very precious in Japan, so the people made the best use of it – both for growing food and for giving pleasure. All Japanese people who could afford it liked to surround their homes with beautiful gardens where they could take gentle exercise, read or entertain.

Japanese gardens were often small, but they were carefully planned to create a landscape in miniature. Each rock, pool, temple or gateway was positioned where it could best be admired, but also where it formed part of a balanced, harmonious arrangement. Japanese designers chose plants to create a garden that would look good during all the different seasons of the year. Zen gardens – made of stones, sand and gravel – contained no plants at all.

Plants to Admire

Artists created and recorded delicate arrangements of blooms and leaves. This scroll-painting of branches, blossom and flowers dates from the 1500s.

Zen Garden

This is part of a Zen Buddhist garden, made of lumps of rock and carefully-raked gravel. Gardens like this were designed to help people pray and meditate in peaceful surroundings.

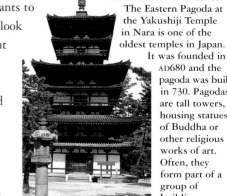

Harmony in Design

The Eastern Pagoda at the Yakushiji Temple in Nara is one of the oldest temples in Japan. It was founded in AD680 and the pagoda was built in 730. Pagodas are tall towers, housing statues of Buddha or other religious works of art. Often, they form part of a group of buildings standing in a garden.

Making an *Ikebana* Arrangement

You will need: vase filled with water, scissors, twig, raffia or string, 2 flowers (with different length stems), a branch of foliage, 2 stems of waxy leaves.

1 Cut the twig so that it can be wedged into the neck of the vase. This will provide a structure to build on and to control the position of the flowers.

2 Remove the twig from the vase. Next, using raffia or string, tie the twig tightly on to the longest flower about halfway down the stem.

3 Place the flower stem in the vase. As you do this, gently slide the twig back into the neck of the vase and wedge it into position as before.

TREES IN MINIATURE

Bonsai is the Japanese art of producing miniature but fully-formed trees. This is achieved by clipping roots and carefully regulating the water supply. Bonsai originated in China, but became popular in Japan around 1500. A tree that might naturally grow to about 6m could end up just 30cm tall after bonsai treatment. Some bonsai trees are grown to achieve a dramatic slanting or twisted shape.

bonsai maple   *bonsai pine*

CHINESE STYLE

The Tenryuji Temple, Kyoto, stands in one of the oldest Buddhist gardens still surviving in Japan. The garden was created before 1300. It is designed in the Chinese style and made of rocks, gravel, water and evergreen plants.

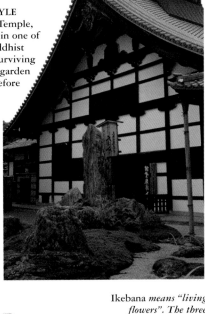

GARDENERS AT WORK

A gardener, his wife and son prepare to plant cedar tree saplings. In the foreground, you can see a wooden bucket for watering plants, and a wooden hoe for digging up weeds. At the back, there are nursery beds where seedlings are carefully tended. Cedar trees were, and still are, popular in Japan. The wood is used in the building of houses and the beautiful trees themselves are used to decorate many gardens.

Ikebana means "living flowers". The three main branches of an arrangement represent heaven, earth and human beings.

4 Add the shorter-stemmed flower to the longer stem. Position it so that it slants forwards. Carefully lean it against the twig and the longer stem.

5 Slip the branch of foliage between the two stems. It should lean out and forward. The foliage should look as though it is a branch growing naturally.

6 Position some waxy leaves at the neck of the vase. *Ikebana* is the arrangement of anything that grows. Foliage is as important as the flowers.

7 Add a longer stem of waxy leaves at the back of the vase. This simple arrangement is typical of those Japanese people have in their homes.

Festivals and Ceremonies

T HE JAPANESE PEOPLE CELEBRATED FESTIVALS (*matsuri*) all year round, but especially during the warm months of spring and summer. Many of these festivals had ancient origins and were connected with farming or to the seasons. Others were linked to Shinto beliefs or to imported Buddhist ideas. There were two main kinds of festival. National holidays, such as New Year, were celebrated throughout Japan. Smaller local festivals were often linked to a Buddhist statue or temple, or to an ancient Shinto shrine.

One of the most important ceremonies was the tea ceremony, first held by Buddhist monks between 1300 and 1500. During the ceremony, the host served tea to his or her guests with great delicacy, politeness and precision.

BOWLS FOR TEA
At a tea ceremony, two types of green tea are served in bowls like these. The bowls are often plainly shaped and simply decorated. According to Zen beliefs, beauty can be found in pure, calm, simple things. Toyotomi Hideyoshi fell out with the tea master Sen no Rikyu over this. Hideyoshi liked tea bowls to be ornate rather than plain.

LOCAL FESTIVAL
A crowd of people enjoy a festival day. Local festivals usually included processions of portable Shinto shrines through the streets. These were followed by lots of noisy and cheerful people.

TEA BOWL
You will need: self-drying clay, cutting board, ruler, modelling tool, cut-out bottom of a plastic bottle (about 10cm in diameter), fine sandpaper, paints, paintbrush, water pot, soft cloth, varnish and brush.

1 Roll out a snake of clay 25cm long and 1cm thick. Starting from the centre, curl the clay tightly into a circle with a diameter of 10cm.

2 Now you have made the base of the bowl, start to build up the sides. Roll out more snakes of clay, 25cm long. Join the pieces by pressing them together.

3 Sculpt the ridges of the coil bowl together using your fingers and modelling tool. Use the bottom of a plastic bottle for support (see step 4).

CHERRY BLOSSOM

This woodblock print shows two women dressed in their best *kimonos* strolling along an avenue of flowering cherry trees. The cherry-blossom festival, called Hanami, was a time to meet friends and enjoy an open-air meal in the spring sunshine. Blossoms appeared in late February in the far south, but not until early May in the colder northern lands of Japan.

BLOSSOM

The Japanese looked forward to the sight of plum blossom emerging, usually in mid February. The plum tree was the first to blossom. In March and April, cherry trees followed suit by producing clouds of delicate pink and white blossom. People hurried to admire the cherry blossom before its fragile beauty faded away. This joyful festival was also tinged with sadness. Spring was the rainy season in Japan and one storm could cause the blossom to fail. The cherry blossom was a reminder that human lives could soon disappear.

plum blossom

cherry blossom

TEA CEREMONY

Hostess and guests sit politely on *tatami* (straw mats) for a Zen tea ceremony. This ritual often lasted for up to four hours. Many people in Japan still hold tea ceremonies, as a way of getting away from hectic modern life.

Design your bowl in a pure, elegant style, like the Zen potters. If you want to add any decoration, make sure that is very simple, too.

4 Roll out another coil of clay 19cm long and 1cm wide. Make it into a circle 8cm in diameter. Join the ends. This will form a stand for the bowl.

5 Turn the bowl over – still using your drinks bottle for support. Join the circular stand to the bottom of the bowl. Mould it on using your fingers.

6 Leave the bowl to dry. Once dry, remove the plastic bottle and sand the bowl gently. Paint the base colour over it. Leave until it is dry.

7 Apply your second colour using a cloth. Lightly dapple paint over the bowl to make it appear like a glaze. Varnish the bowl inside and out.

Glossary

A

Ainu The original inhabitants of northern Japan.

akido A Japanese martial art in which players try to overbalance their opponents.

ancestor A family member who died long ago.

ashigaru A samurai (warrior) with a low rank.

B

barter The exchange of goods for others of equal value.

Buddha The name (meaning 'the enlightened one') given to Siddhartha Gautama, an Indian prince who lived around 500BC. He taught a new philosophy, based on seeking peace (*nirvana*).

Buddhism A world faith, based on the Buddha's teachings.

bugaku An ancient dance form that was popular at the court of the Japanese emperor.

bunraku Japanese puppet plays.

bushido A strict code of brave, honourable behaviour, meant to be followed by samurai (warriors).

C

clan A group of people related to each other by ancestry or marriage.

D

daimyo A nobleman or warlord.

dynasty The successive generations of a ruling family.

G

garrison A fort or similar place that is guarded by a troop of soldiers. The word garrison can also refer to the troop of soldiers.

geta Wooden clogs, designed to keep feet dry in wet weather.

guilds Groups of skilled workers who checked quality standards, trained young people and looked after old and sick members.

H

haiku A short poem, containing 17 syllables. Haiku were popular after about AD1600.

Haniwa Clay figures that were buried in ancient Japanese tombs. They are a very important source of evidence about early Japan.

I

ikat A weaving technique. The threads are dyed in many different colours then woven together to create complicated and beautiful patterns.

ikebana The art of flower-arranging that is practised in Japan.

inro A small, decorated box, worn hanging from the belt. Originally, *inro* were designed for storing medicines.

inscribed Something that is carved on stone or another similar hard material.

J

Jomon An early hunter-gatherer civilisation in Japan. It originated in about 10,000BC.

K

kabuki Popular plays, performed in Japan from about AD1600. They were fast-moving and loud.

kami The Japanese holy spirits.

kana The name for the Japanese method of writing.

kanji The picture-symbols that were used for writing Japanese before about AD800.

kendo A martial art in which players fight one another with bamboo swords.

kimono A loose robe with wide sleeves, worn by both men and women.

kuzu A plant with a fleshy root that is dried and used in traditional medicine.

L

lacquer A shiny varnish, made from the sap of trees.

litter A portable bed.

loom A piece of equipment used to weave cloth.

M

mausoleum A burial chamber.

mica A flaky, shiny metal.

millet A grass-like plant that produces edible seeds.

monsoon Winds that blow at particular seasons of the year in south Asia, bringing heavy rain.

mosaics Tiny pieces of colourful stone, shell or glass that are used to make pictures or to decorate objects.

mother-of-pearl The beautiful shiny coating that forms on the inside of an oyster shell.

N

nape The back of the neck.

netsuke Small toggles, carved from ivory and used to attach items to belts.

noh A serious, dignified drama that originated in Japan in around AD1300.

O

obi A wide sash, worn only by women.

omikashi A portable shrine.

P

pagoda A tall tower, usually part of a Buddhist temple.

peninsula An area of land surrounded by water on three sides, making it almost like an island.

pillow book A collection of short notes and writings, rather like a diary.

plate-armour Protective clothing made of overlapping plates of metal.

R

ramie A plant rather like flax, used to make clothing.

regent Someone who rules a country on behalf of another person.

S

sake Rice wine.

samurai Well-trained warriors.

scroll-painting A painting on a long roll of paper.

shamisen A three-stringed musical instrument.

shinden A large, single-storey house in Japan.

Shinto An ancient Japanese religion, known as the 'way of the gods', based on honouring holy spirits.

shoen A private estate in the Japanese countryside.

shogun A Japanese army commander. From 1185-1868, shoguns ruled Japan.

shrine A holy place, used for Shinto worship.

silken Made of silk.

sumo A type of wrestling popular in Japan.

surcoat A long, loose tunic worn over armour.

T

tachi The long sword that was carried by a samurai.

tanbo Flooded fields where rice was grown.

tatami A mat that covers the floor, woven from reeds.

tenshu The tall central tower of a castle.

terracotta Baked clay.

threshing Separating grains of wheat or rice from their stalks.

tofu Bean-curd – a nourishing food made from the pulp of crushed soya beans.

torii The traditional gateway to a Shinto shrine.

U

uji A clan.

W

waka Elegant poetry, popular at the emperor's court.

winnowing Separating grains of wheat and rice from their papery outer layer, called chaff.

Y

yoke A long piece of wood or bamboo, used to help carry heavy loads. The yoke was placed across the shoulders and a load was hung from each end to balance it.

Z

Zen A branch of the Buddhist faith that was popular among the samurai.

Index